The Aerialist Will Not Be Performing

The Aerialist Will Not be Performing

Ekphrastic poems and flash fiction
To the art of Steven Schroeder

By

Robert L. Dean, Jr.

Acknowledgements

The author gratefully acknowledges the editors and staff of the following publications, in which versions of these poems appeared, sometimes in different forms or under different titles:

The Ekphrastic Review: "Aftermath," "Leap of Faith," "When Icarus turns ninety."
KYSO Flash: "Ghost Town," "Ripple Effect," "Trinity," Trouble the Water," "Windmill."
MacQueen's Quinterly: "Dancing in the Eye," "Fall from Grace," "The One the Brothers Grimm Left Out," "What I Remember," "What is the Frequency, Kenneth?"

Cover Art: Steven Schroeder
Book Design: Tim Kehn

Turning Plow Press

ISBN: 978-0-578-65642-7

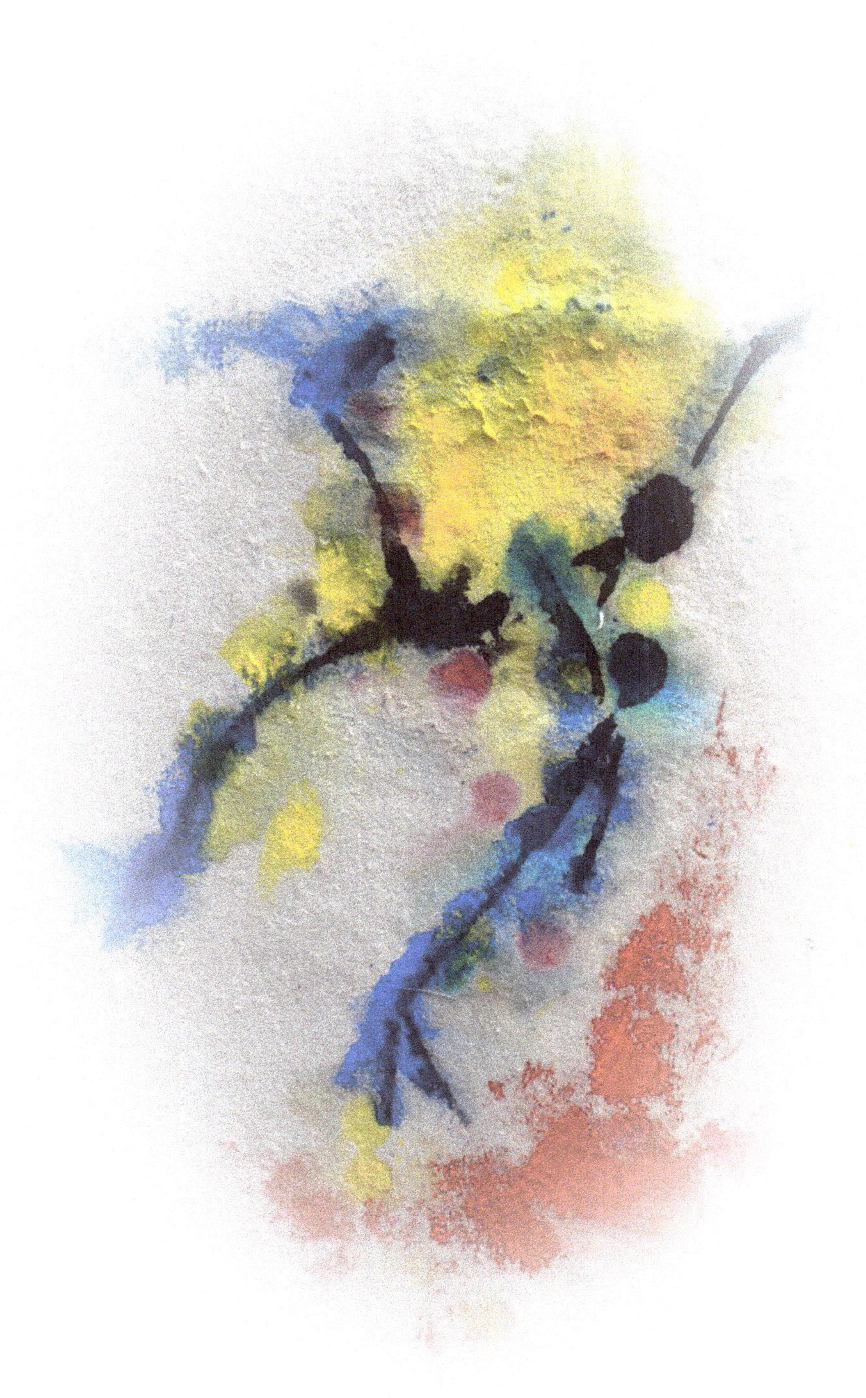

and now, all here and nows, are neither damning nor
fortuitous; they simply are. You will ponder these poems long
after you close the book.

— Ann Howells
former editor, *Illya's Honey*
author of *So Long As We Speak Their Names*

    Robert Dean's second book, a vigorous, rich gathering
of ekphrastic poems and flash fiction written to the paintings
of Steven Schroeder, exudes a Zen sensibility tautly attuned to
the surface silence of the paintings. Dean's vulnerable voice
forges past deep elegies of nothingness and death to reach a
horizon of hope that grounds and embraces Schroeder's
representational and abstract art. In Dean's hands, ekphrastic
metamorphoses into the ecstatic, displaying an imaginative
prowess, and addressing the reader with sage spiritual advice.
His deft use of poetic devices – especially repetition –
permeates his verse with a hypnotic cadence. He brings forth
the shimmering essence of each painting, and his flash fictions
provide a concise layer of narrative and drama. "Aftermath"
may be the best example of Dean's talents. The poem plunges
into a loss of love, its diction direct yet heartbreaking, its
atmosphere: gloom. Yet here, painting and poem echo back in
harmony.

— Arlice W. Davenport
poet and retired Books Page editor for *The Wichita Eagle*

Contents

To Anna
who told me once
aloneness is a good thing

"And if life and death are companions to each other, then what is there to be anxious about?"

Part of the Yellow Emperor's answer to Knowledge, concerning how to know the Way. Section twenty-two of the *Chuang Tzu*, translated by Burton Watson.

Part One

Steps

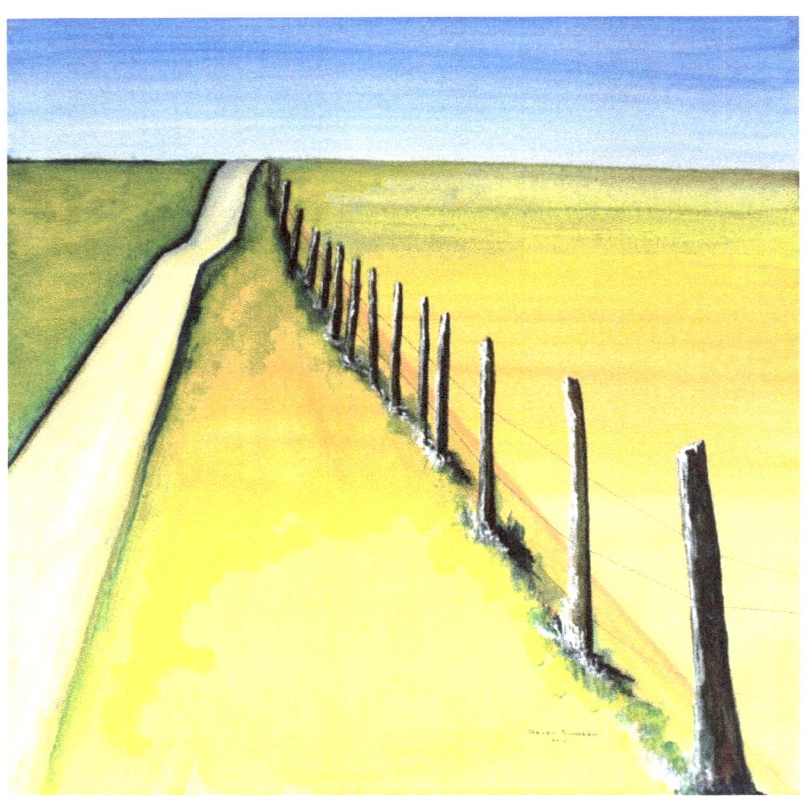

between the lines

Along This Road

Traveler, do not tarry.
Horizons are never
as distant as they seem,

and, just beyond this
one, or the next, I am
waiting. There is a little

inn and once you arrive,
though you suppose you do not
know me, we shall sup.

Traveler, wherever
you are from, wherever
you are headed, whatever

burdens you carry, I will
ease them, take the half,
more, today, tomorrow.

Traveler, whoever
you are is of no
consequence, nor

I, unless we
walk this road together,
for there is no other

and the fence keeps
no one out and
no one in, you see

how it converges
with your destination
though you know not

what awaits. Oh traveler,
I have left these guideposts
just for you. Take my

hand, the few
pennies I possess,
the rod and staff

upon which
your name is inscribed,
the bread and wine.

Oh traveler, do not
let the sun beat you down,
the miles blister your

heart, the solitude
steal your soul.
The way ahead

is clear
of clouds. I have
swept them

from this threshold
in anticipation
of you. Traveler,

do not tarry
long

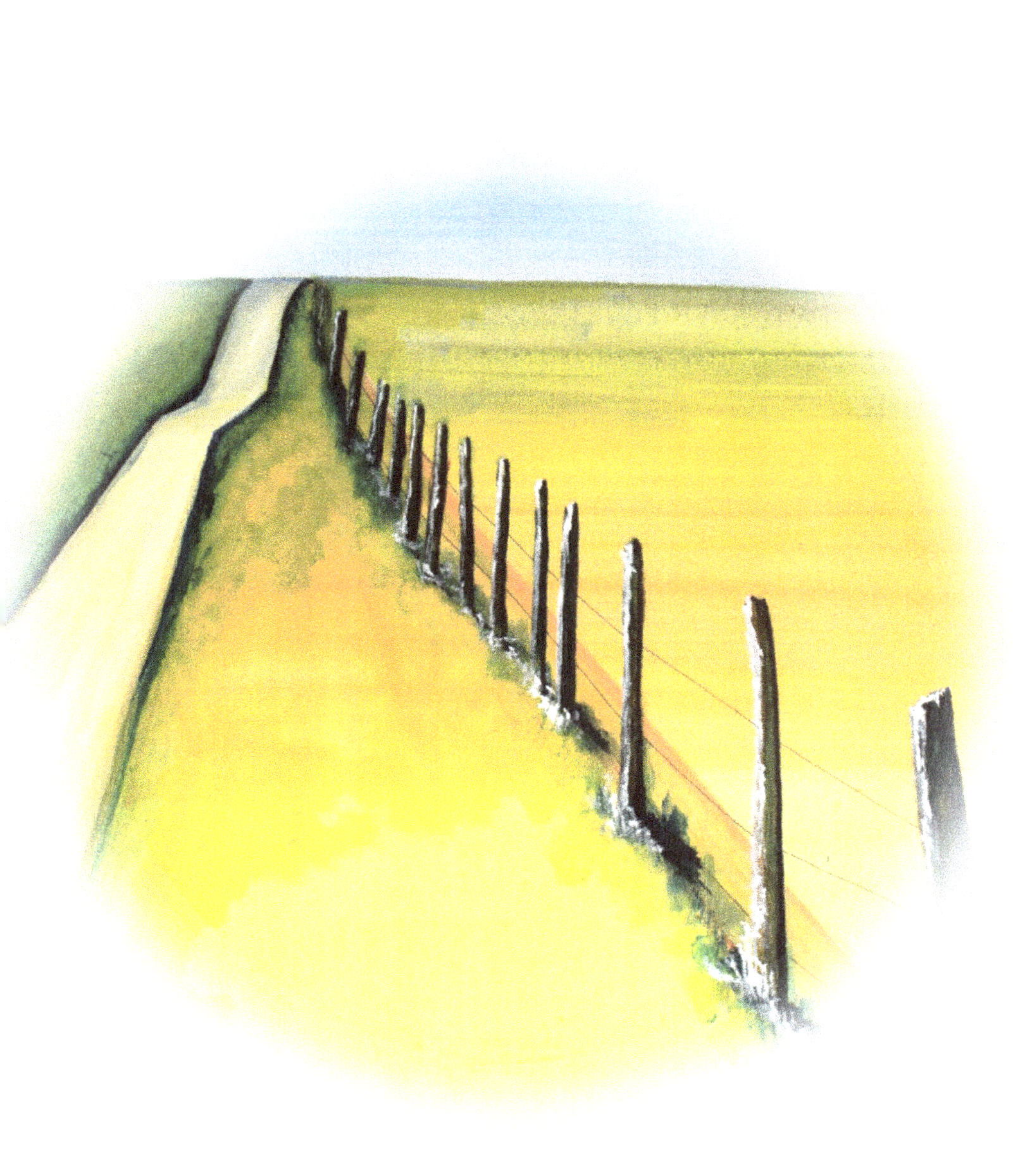

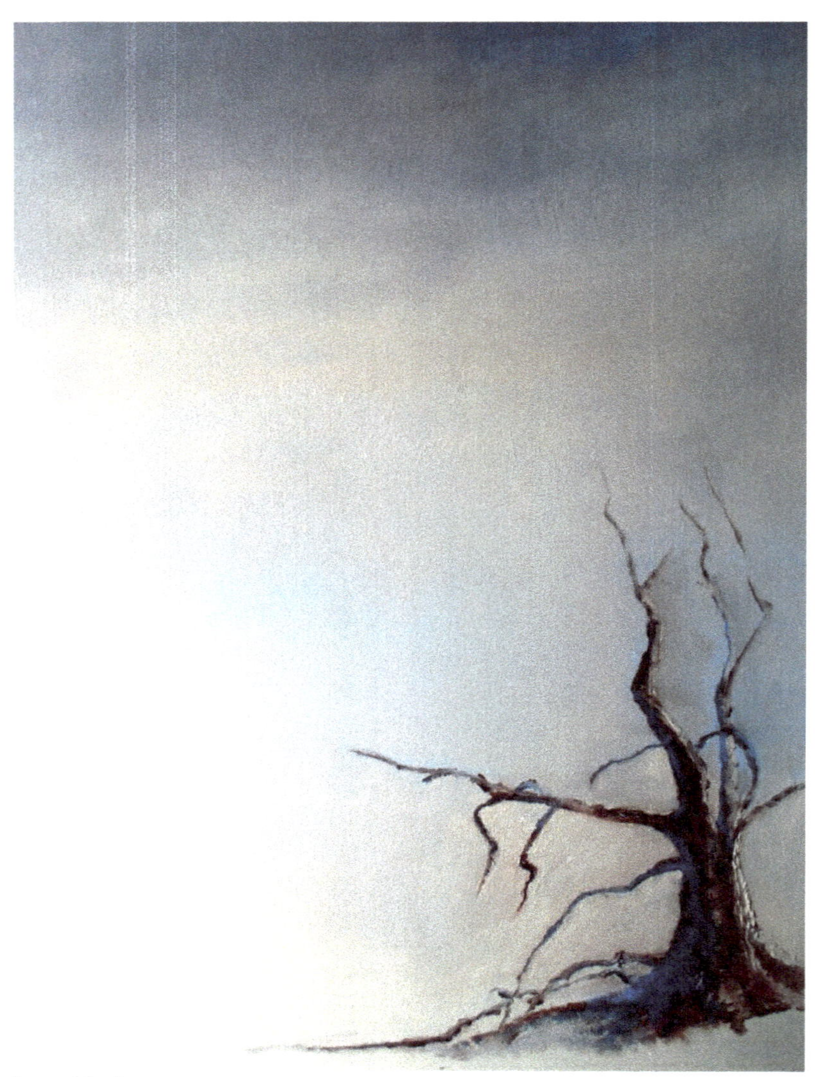

leap of faith

Leap of Faith

We reach out
barren armed
in our aloneness

probe with one long
bony finger
the void

the stuff of our
dreamless days
firmly rooted in

nothing
on the edge of
nothing

thrust up
naked hallelujahs
beseeching

the sky oh the sky
will bless us
if we can but

see it
take that
first step

into other, which is of course
just more
of us

out there
somewhere
everywhere

coming home
to where we
never left.

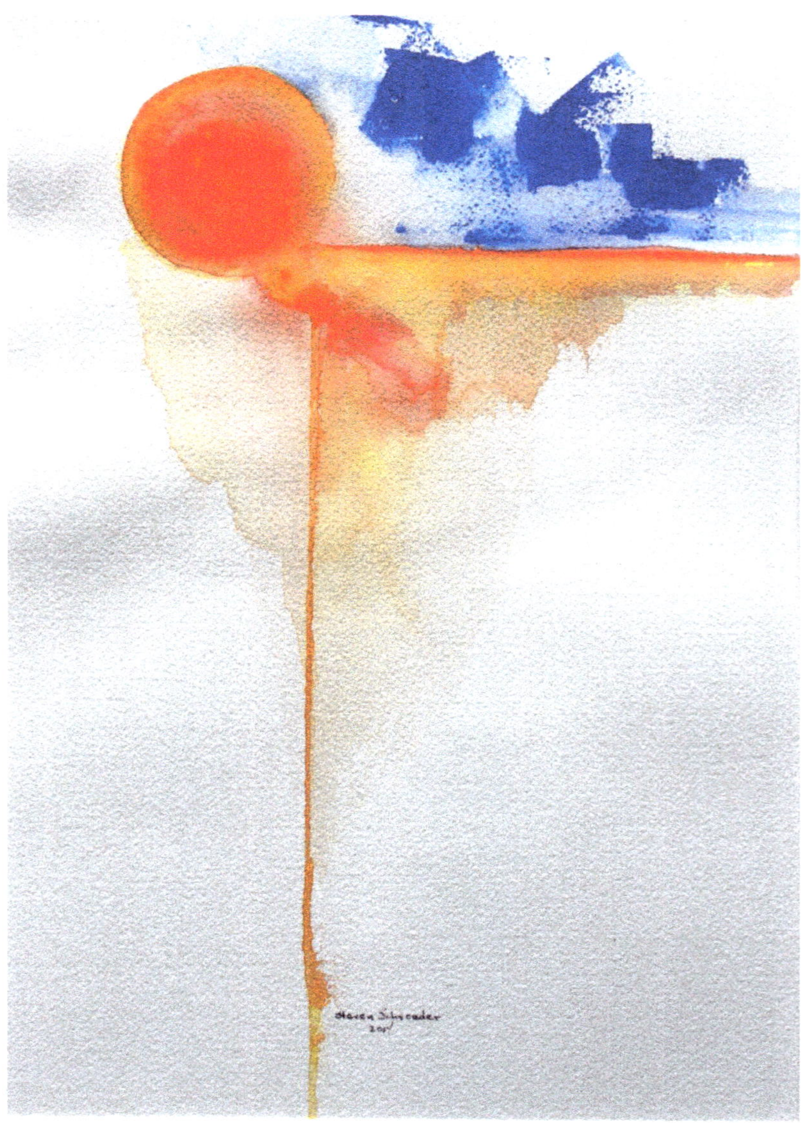

sunset

How it Ends

I have stared too long
into the light, I cannot see
the darkness coming

hear it creeping up
behind me, what Sisyphus
is it that pushes the day

off the edge of forever
will it ever
roll back up

into the bit of blue
all that's left of
the sky we knew

as children, or are those
ship's sails, the Flying
Dutchman perhaps, shadowed in

the doldrums, tacking into
a breathless fire-balled
future, crying out *ahoys*

to voyagers long since dead
such a long list
I wait for my name

on the edge of my seat
bracing for the race
to catch tomorrow

before it is swallowed
by the void, before
it is lost forever

and I am doomed
to sail uncharted
the dead seas

of my own creation
can't you hear me calling
through the last of the

falling lignum vitae
leaves
No? Nor can I.

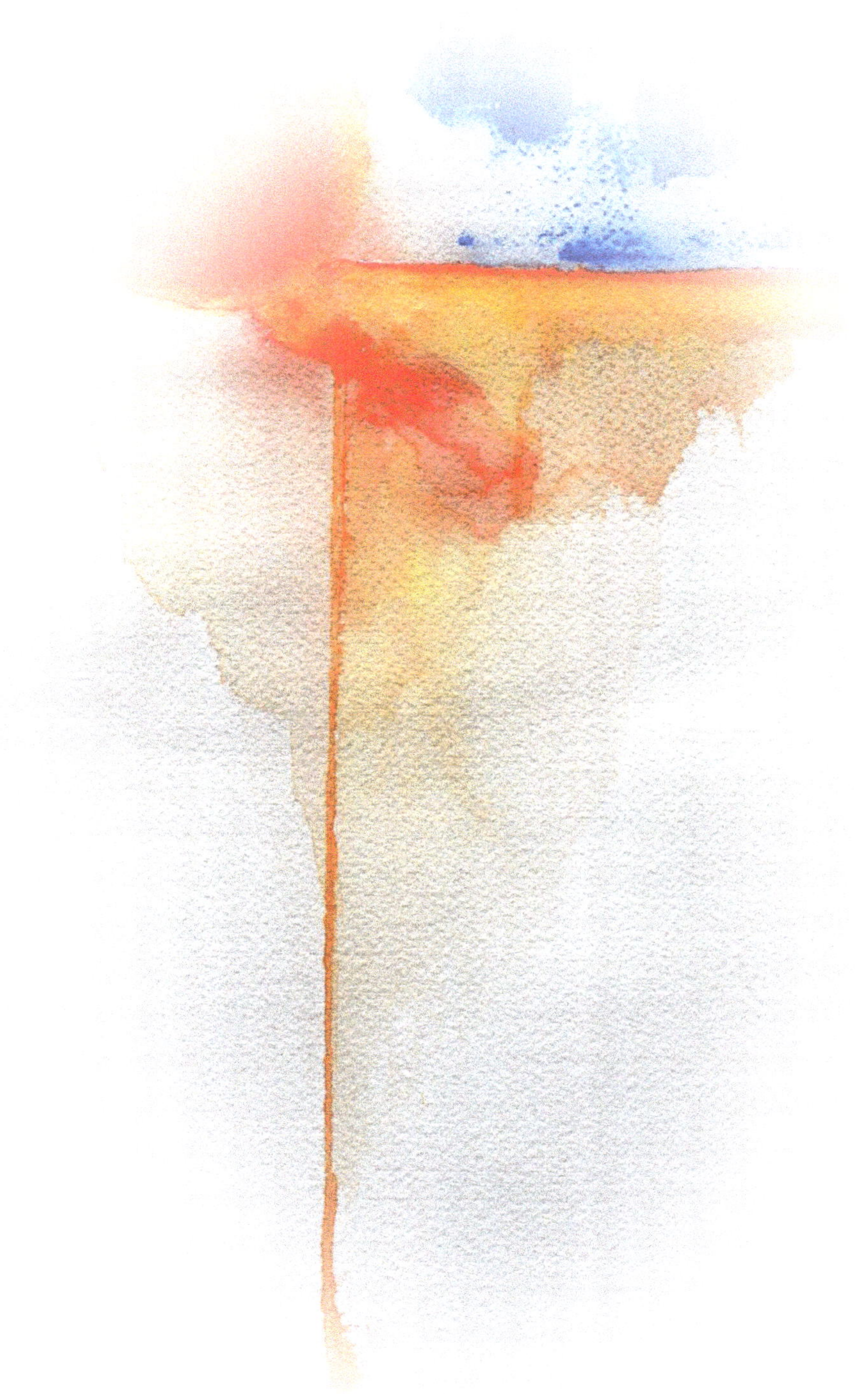

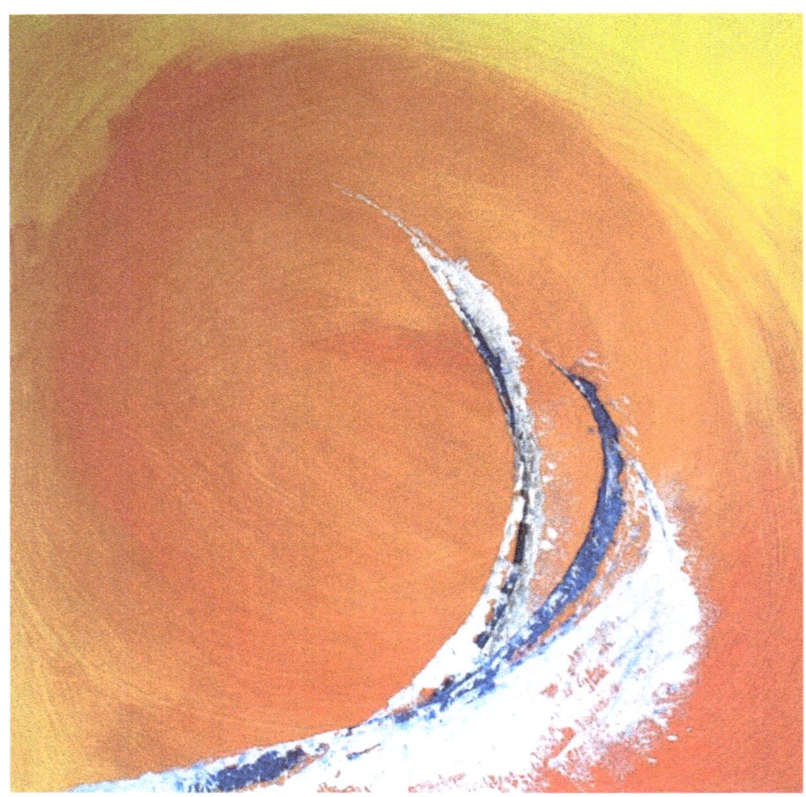

flight

When Icarus turns ninety

it's just another day at the Y
and at first I don't notice him
pedaling the bike machine

at the distant end of the row
facing the battery of big screens
ESPN, CNN, FOX, HGTV

keeping us grounded
in the events of this Earth
until something catches

the corner of my eye
—a flash of wing maybe—
and there he is, smaller

than I expected, shriveled,
hunched over the machine
pedaling as if he had

all the time in the world
no hurry, what's the rush
the light glinting off his

bald pate, eyes exploring
the floor beneath him
wing-shorn, unless that

hump on his back
bears more than
ancient vertebrae

incognito, yes, wouldn't
you be, with his backstory
all that youthful hubris

and Ovid reporting you
dead, your own father
buying into it, Bruegel

depicting your ignominious
end, feet kicking up from
the sea that would not bear

your name if word got out
about those Samian fishermen
and their nets, no, the follies

of youth are best forgot
so I can't help but wonder
when I see him later

slogging his snail-paced way
through the parking lot
towards a brand new

sunburst yellow Corvette
if maybe there's some hope
for me, for all of us

if maybe youth
is a state of grace
a frame of mind

if only
we just keep pedaling

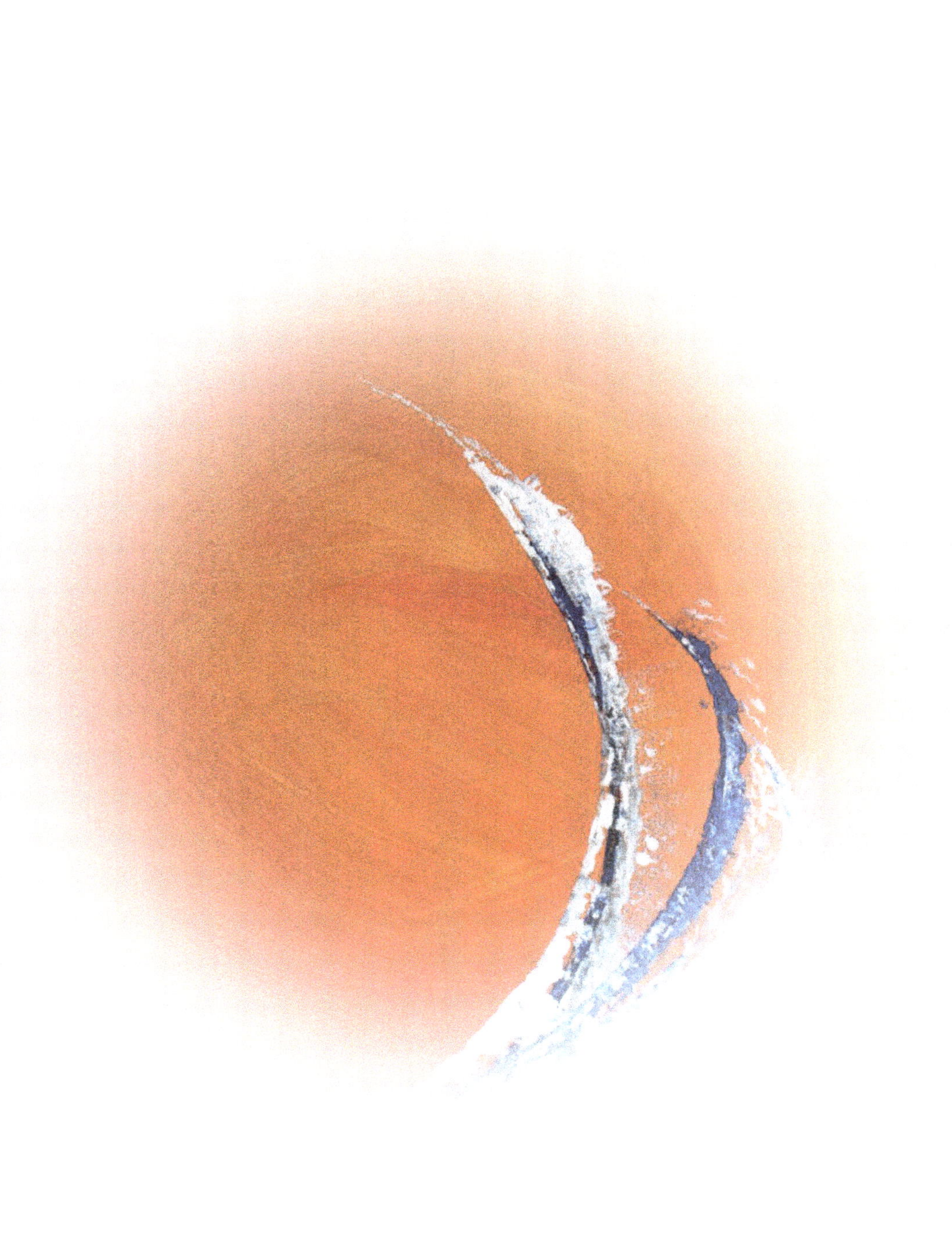

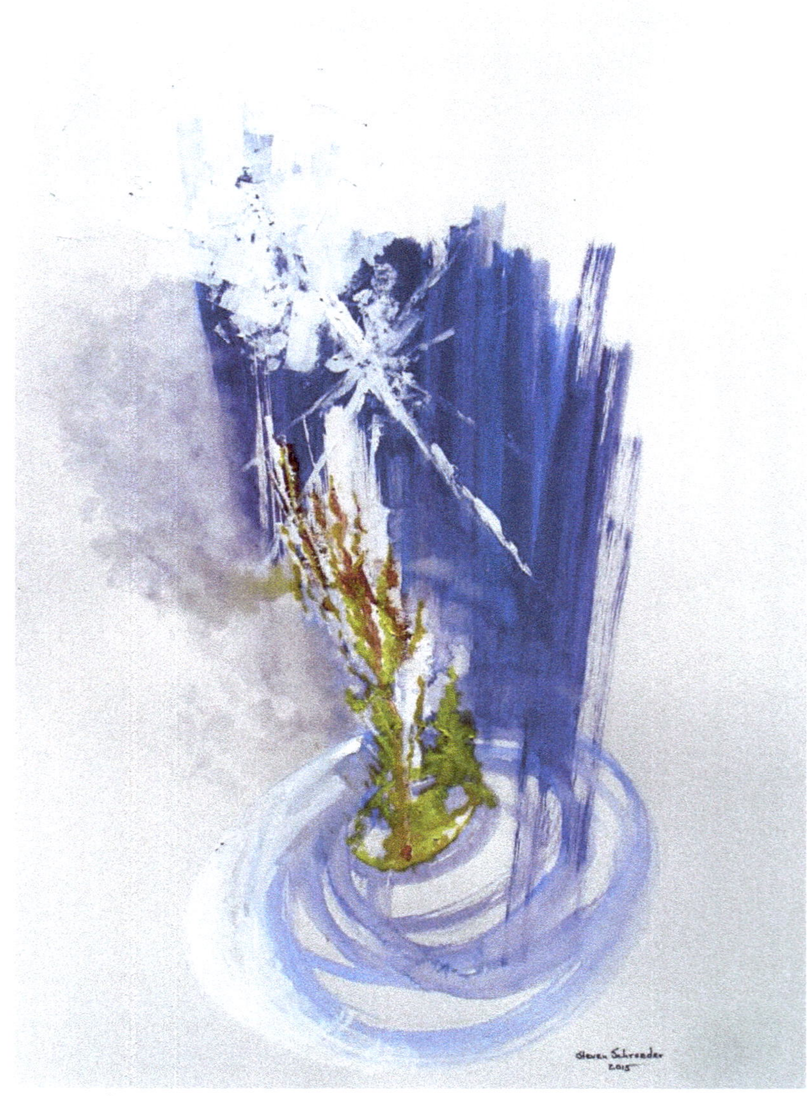

water circles

Ripple Effect
A haibun

More swim, she says, tugging her grandmother's hand back towards the pool. *More swim.* But grandmother stands firm, or, rather, tugs in the direction of the door. Places to go, people to see, or words to that effect, spill from her lips. One of life's little wars, breaking out in the lobby of the YMCA. I try to remain neutral, conjure an Alpine Swiss meadow, skirt the edge of the battlefield. The tiny aquanaut's blue eyes catch mine: *More swim?* she asks, her face awash with sudden hope; for, after all, isn't that what we all want? More? More of everything, especially all fruits forbidden? Grandmother wants more of whatever's outside. The woman with the hijab and sensible sneakers just entering wants to run more marathons without people staring as she passes. The attendant behind the counter with the bulging biceps wants more people to notice his bulging biceps. The elderly couple holding hands while pedaling the bike machines want more time before one hand or the other goes empty. The cars in the lot want to drive all the streets in the city. The city wants to annex more of the world. The world wants more world, the sun more sun, the universe more universe.

Swim? The index finger of her free hand between hopeful lips, I her longed-for lifeguard.

And suddenly I am four and treading water, watching in awe as ripples spread out from me to the farthest reaches of the pool, to the tile where mom and dad stand, snapping Polaroids and getting the latest on my progress from the bronzed instructor, the sting of chlorine lingering in my eyes. And I want more, my hands moving in bigger, faster circles. Oh, so much more.

The Polaroids have long since faded into blurs of light and
dark. The bronze god is a dim legend, the navigation of water
bodies a lost cause.

I pull down the brim of my battered Royals cap, heave a
grandfatherly sigh: *Not today, sweetheart.* Turn away from the
broken heart of a face, hear the war resume as I push through
the door and into whatever more awaits.

brown leaf
fall pond shivers
sends word

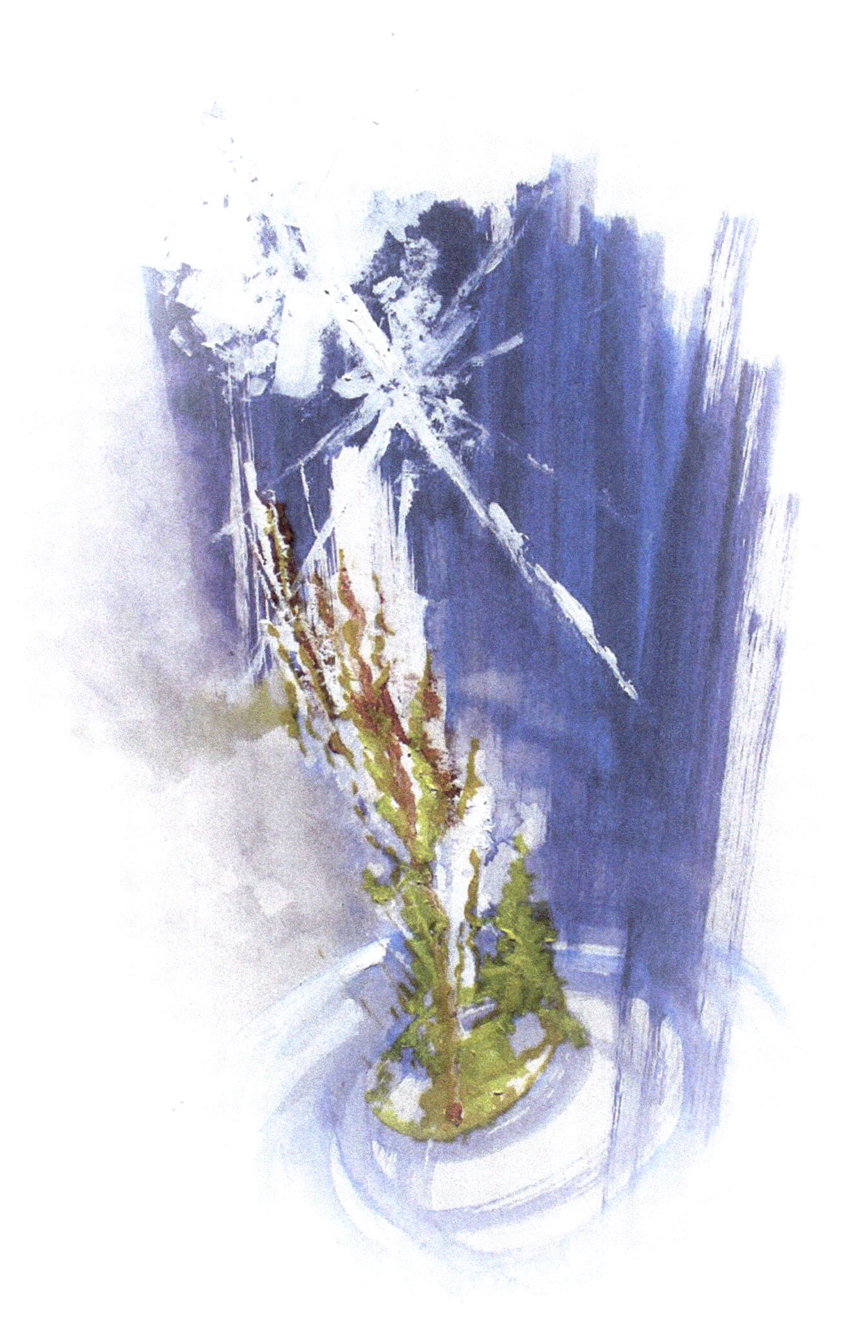

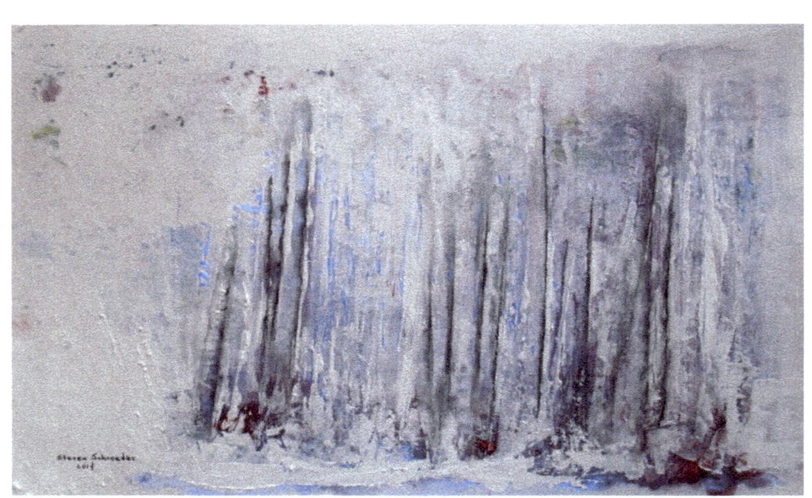

forest

The Heart in Winter

When you leave, you take the sun and the long leisure days,
                    the green shoots of birthing hope,
                    the pulse of short nights hot
                    with the skin and scent of us,
                    the pearlescent voyeur moon.
When you leave, the pear blossoms fall like frozen tears,
                    tulips droop their heads, hyacinths
                    trumpet unceasing caesura.
When you leave, the Johnny-Jump-ups in the window box
                    shave their beards in mourning,
                    Barrett Brownings number
                    no more orange-cupped love.
When you leave, black spruce burst through the floor
                    of wreckage we once called
                    home, bedsheets hoar to lichen.

Like a fox, I ball up, legs under belly, tail over nose,
                    insulate against the tundra
                    of absence, the permafrost
                    of silent rooms, empty closets.
Like a fox, I tunnel and burrow, face my maze-mouthed
                    den to where your warmth once was, hope
                    for a revenant, a sign, a whiff of spoor.
Like a fox, I hunt the lemming, even to the edge of the cliff,
                    and, none too soon I fear, beyond,
                    or, in the lean times, my feces
                    becomes my prey.
Like a fox, I pad my way across the polar floes from
                    desolation to desolation, sniff
                    carcass after carcass, know
                    in my marrow bones
                    it is only a killing of time.

Like a fox, I am become ghost in this tomb of ice and wood,
            only the crimson drip
            of my wounding
            visible from tree to tree to tree.

Like a fox
the heart in winter
when you leave

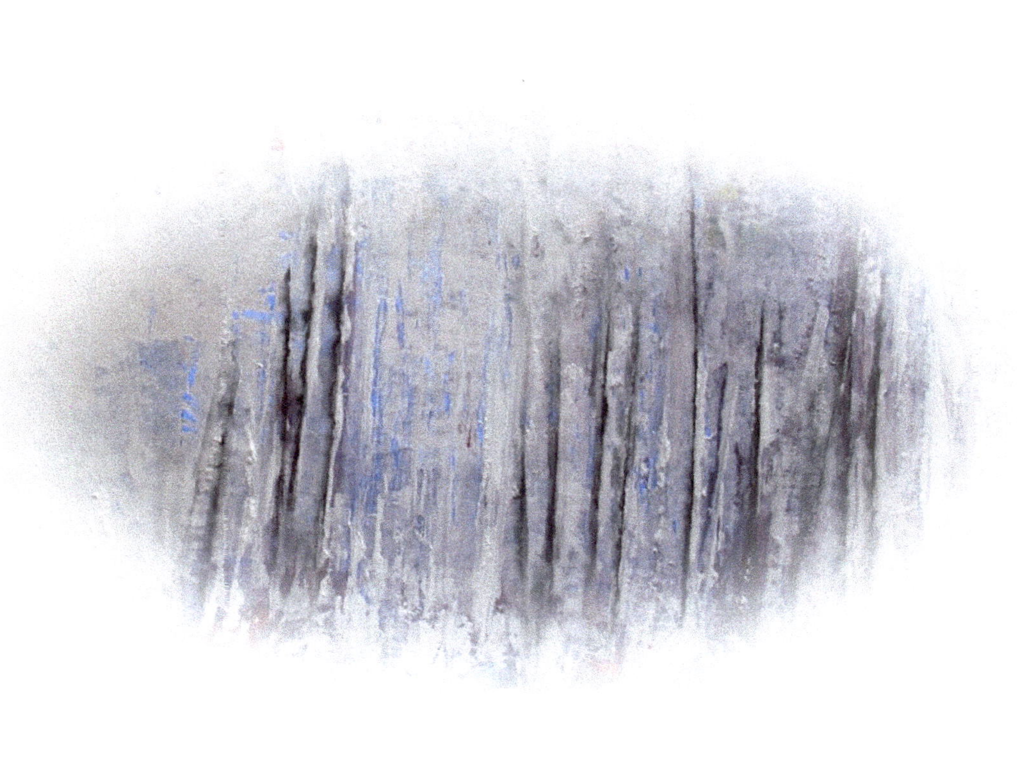

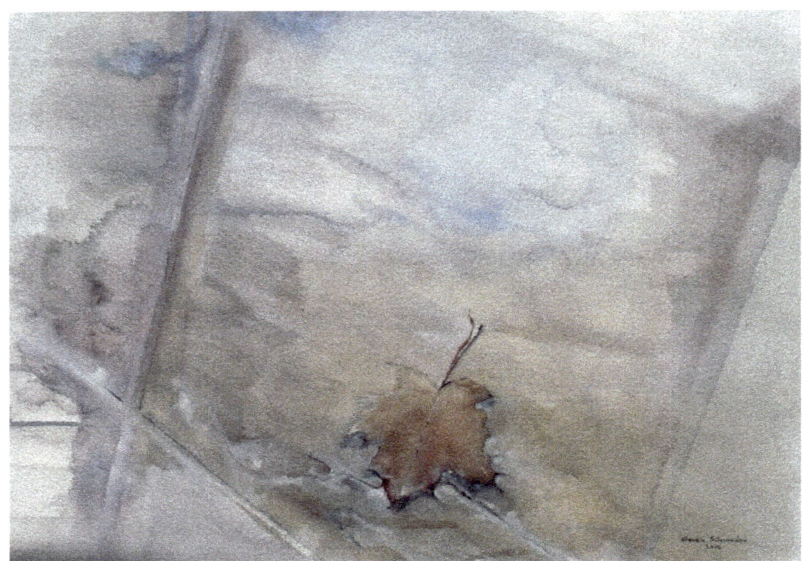

the order of things

Aftermath

Just yesterday, it seems,
the world breathed fire and gold
and we, arms interwoven,

paused here

one bold blue October morning,
gazed out

at the changeling sugar maple
with our initials so impulsively emblazoned, no
caution taken

for the birthing of snows,
the winter winds brittling flesh,
piercing the bones with

cold sharp words

on the order of all things,
no thought

for the shedding of skins,
coats of many colors shrugged off,
no thought

that one of us would be
ever on the outside
looking in.

Better, perhaps,

that this glass be
wholly empty
instead of

half full,

beating tears of a phantom heart
fast fading,

awaiting only
the kiss
of December's lips

to smother the flicker out,
to usher in the season of last, lost things.

Listen: love skitters
like a dead soul
into the darkling deep,

not even a sigh of spring
to keep it company.

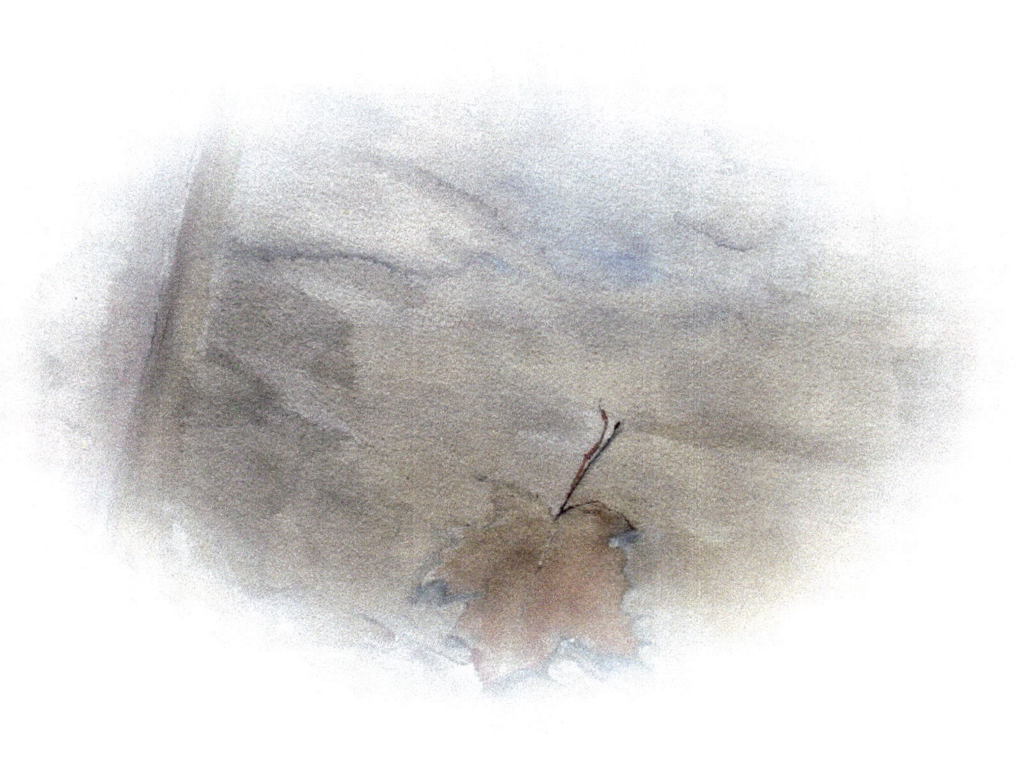

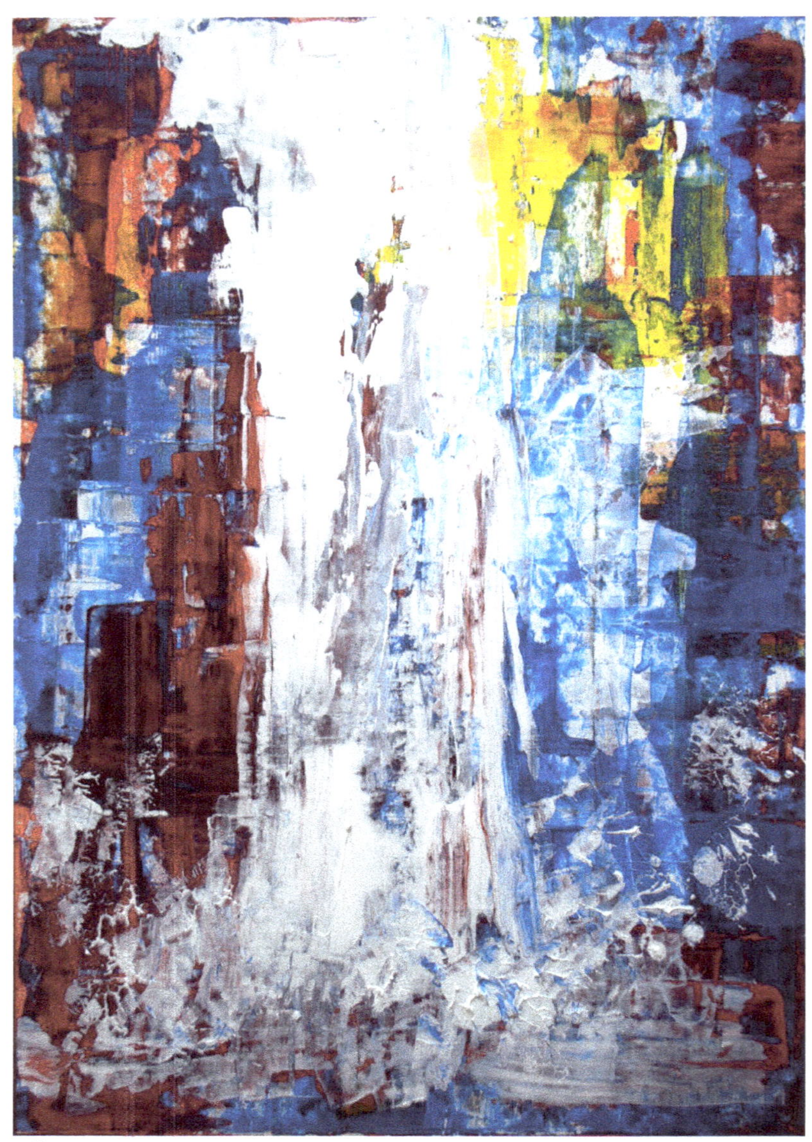

fall

Not Niagara

We come here to consummate
divorce, separation, spats,
arguments, disagreements,
dissatisfaction with the
status quo, quarrels with

our inner selves. The spillover
of bruised and bloody
choler provides all the
native color we can stomach,

the heat of our hearts
is more than a match
for the campfire spark

of others of our kind, caught up
in the anger of a moment,
the slow burn of long term

resentment. O dearly un-
beloved, we are gathered here today

to say our vows at the foot of
this veil of tears we have
hitched ourselves to, assemble

rickety barrels of self-pity
with which to adventure the torrent's brink,
string untaught wires high above
the scratch eroding our

thin skin, search in vain
for mislaid beams of balance.

The inner ear roar of ourselves
drowns out all cautions,
warnings, voices of
reason, reconciliation,
compromise. No by God!

we shout, stepping out into
the void. We have anted up
for this and we will get
our money's worth,

play this hand to the end,
even though it's
the dead man's hand
we dealt ourselves
off the bottom of the deck,

even if the boulders we have
shouldered into place
at the misty end
of the journey shatter

everything
we once loved.

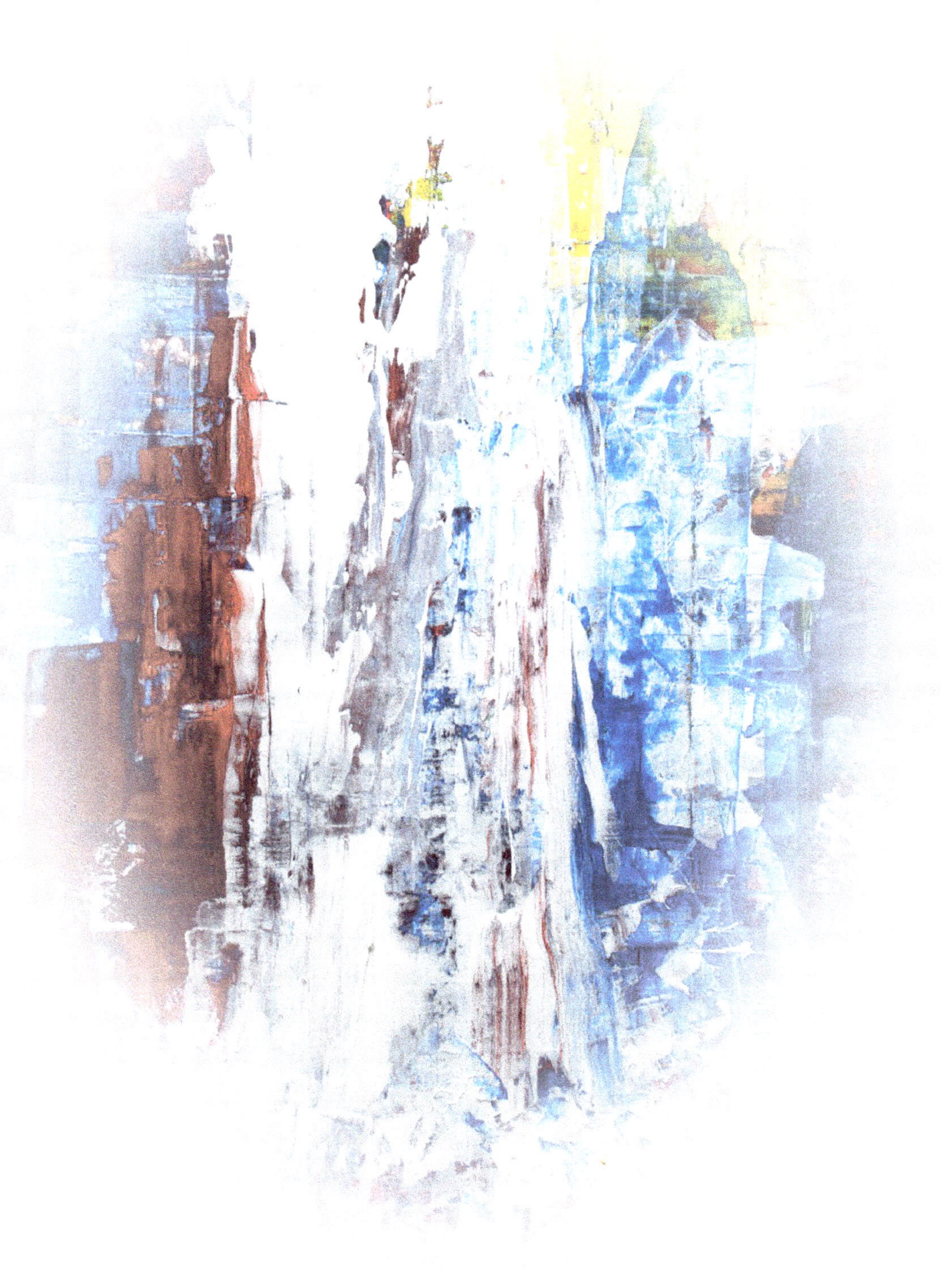

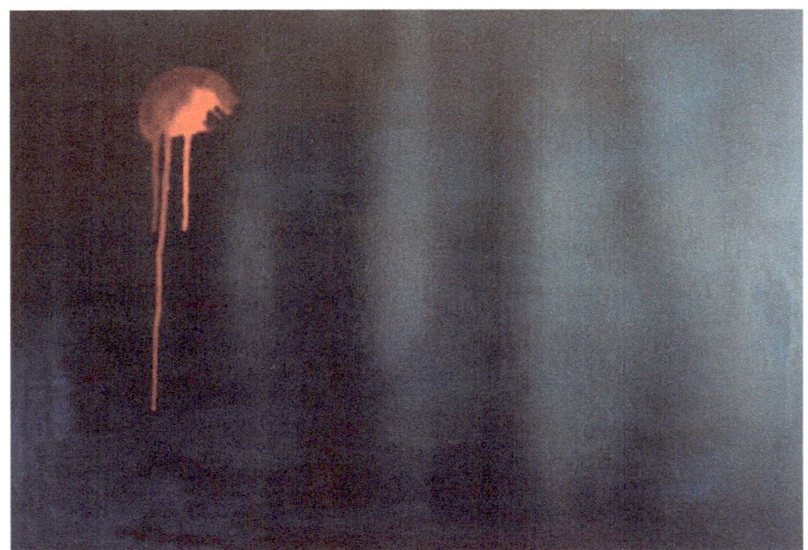

longing stains the silence of the future

Still Life with Roman Noir

So, this is how it ends. Which one of us pulled the trigger, which one of us is bleeding, doesn't matter. What matters is the dark, how it lasts forever, how it's been there all along, finger twitching on cold metal, how we both rushed to meet it, how it anticipates the second, final, shot.

That September day I stepped out of the Parisian rain into the little bistro on *Rue des Martyrs* and found you sitting in the corner shadows drinking absinthe, how our eyes first met, yours deep as wells, I like a pebble, falling, falling, it was there then, while we talked about nothing in particular, there while we walked under your red umbrella up the *Montmartre* steps to *Sacré Coeur* as you told me the story of Saint Denis, who, decapitated by the Romans, carried his head the length of the street before dying, there as you dipped slender red-nailed fingers into the holy water font, signed the cross over your head and breast, whispered *God the Son, Redeemer of the World, have mercy on us*, there at *Cimitière de Montmartre* as you pointed out Falconetti's grave, told me *I want to burn like her*, something I did not understand until days later, when, at your *logement in Avenue Victor Hugo*, you played the DVD of Dryer's *La Passion de Jeanne d'Arc*, and I saw the burning, the terrible burning, the much too realistic burning, and remembered you had told me on the way down the steps from the basilica *There is no God, no redemption in this world or the next*, the rain spattering like muted bullets on the arched pongee dome you held us under, and how I'd wondered at the contradiction in your words and actions for a moment only.

And that night—this night—after I have entered you for the second time, you take the Beretta from your nightstand, momentarily dazzling in the undraped moonlight, and say, matter-of-factly: *One of us will want this someday, don't you think?*

How prophetic you can be. How well you know me. How little time it took.

You lay the Beretta on the sheet between us, release the safety, say, *Tell me about them.* And I do. All those loved and lost. Discarded like so many decapitated heads. All the funeral pyres I've lit: London, Rome, New York. All the saints I've slaughtered. How the darkness never leaves.

The moon slips behind a cloud and you look at me and a shadow something like a smile passes over your face and you say, your breath a flame licking my ear: *They are here, now. Yours. Mine. They will never show us mercy. Never leave us. This is where it ends. Fire that sheds no light is a cold, dead, thing.* And, as always—as you were in London, Rome, New York—you are right.

I reach for the gun, find your hand already there. For less time than it takes an angel to fall, fire lights the night.

standard time 2: light rain

Cold Harbor

This is the zone where
light is not saved,
where the sun goes
to die.

Here the climate
drizzles round the clock,
the dull steel sky
never forges
heaven sweeping anvils.

We swarm into port
like conquistadores,
plant skull and crossbones
in the boot-sucking mud,
despoil the nothing
we have undiscovered.

Slow sky drips wear us down,
bit by skin sloughing bit.

We are become nubbins,
stunted after the fact
of being, watching the bone-bags
of what-could-have-beens
swirl down the gutter.

Our hearts, our hearts, where did we
pack our hearts? Or were they left behind
on the far shore, the point of no return?
Thrown overboard with the horses
in the latitudes of blister-lipped stillness?

We have come to save, we lie through
scurvied teeth, hoping the dank absence
is listening, crossing ourselves
with crying fingers, praying that,
at last, we will be believed.

We gape our mouths, turn face-
heavenward, drink in the
Jesus wept tears,
hope for a miracle.

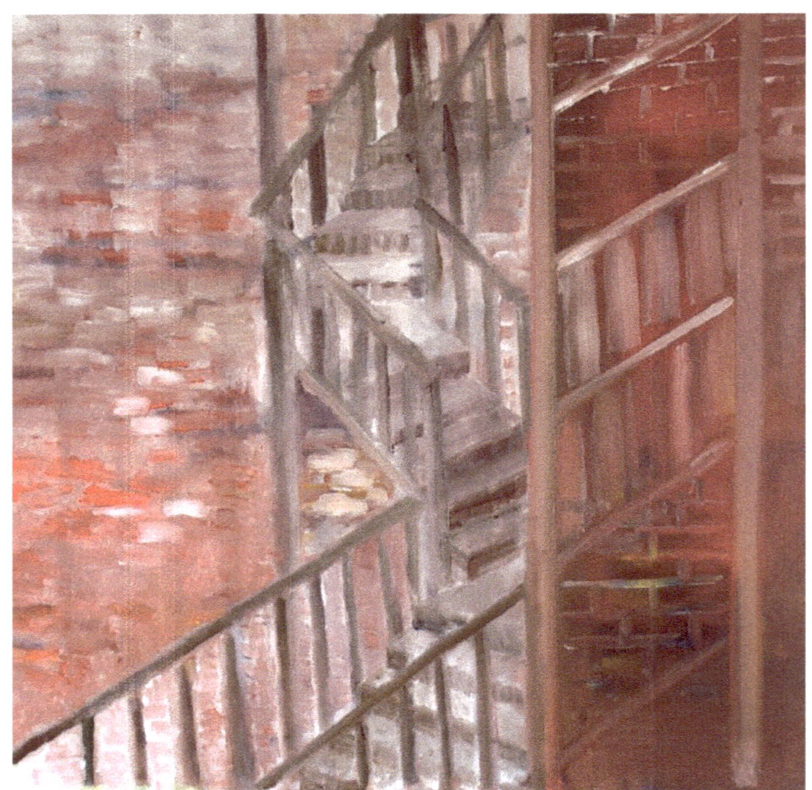

city

Steps

The bricks blush still
remembering the heat
of us in the night

we never made it
to the top, past the
first landing, oh

we were a show
alright, had anyone
opened a back alley

window, stepped out
on the fire escape
to take in the night air

both of us
with our jeans down
bodies wrapped

around bodies, stars
falling all around us
and today as I pack

the half of us
which is mine
one last time

and forever, out
of this apartment
I hear the echo

of bodies fallen
see the absurdity
of the thing, the

Escher-esque quality
of ascent, how
your steps led one way

and mine another
how there was
never anything

at the top anyway
just a suggestion
the naked want

of a door.

Part Two

The One the Brothers Grimm Left Out

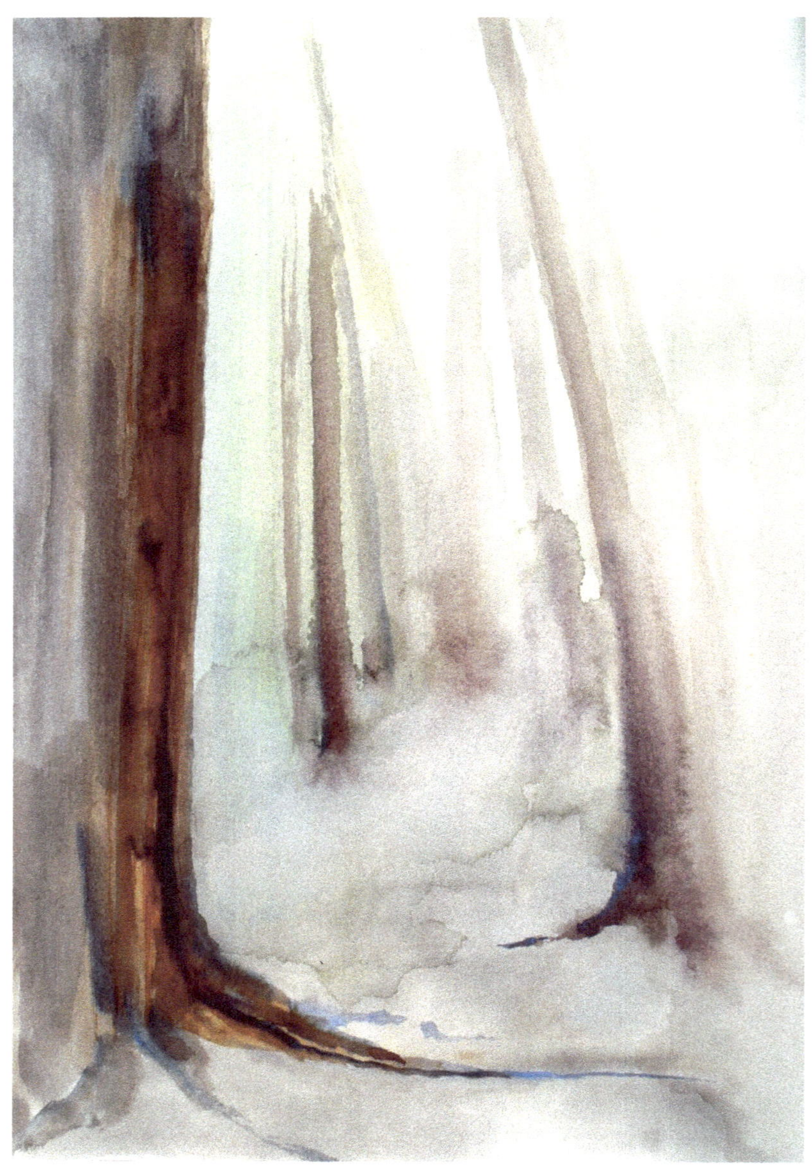

black alders, gray water

Us Previous

This is the path
to Nowhere. It leads
through the
Forest of Nothing.
We know this path,
we've taken it
before. Once we
get there—once
we do not arrive
at no destination—
there is
no way out, no
path back. Return
is not
an option
—and yet,
here we are
once again,
the tracks of
us previous
washed away,
déjà vu alders
leaning in,
whispering
foggy warning.

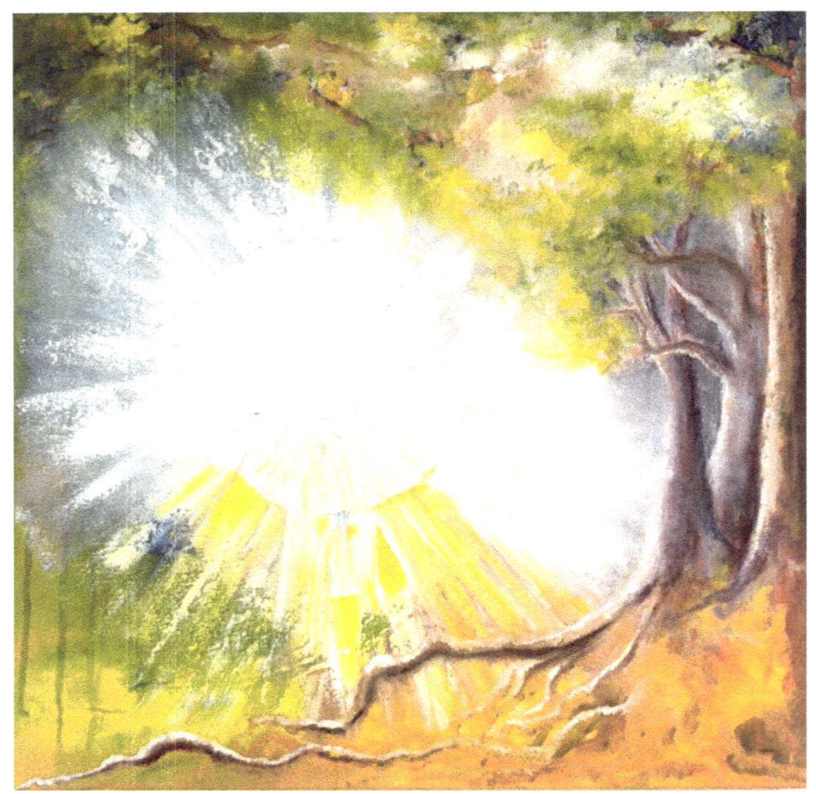

tree of life 8

Tree of Life

Heaven has come to ground.
Life walks on tendrils in flux,
snakes out tentative bowers of
autumn-turning arms, bursts
into flames at the root.

Here is what we forfeit
in all its celestial glory,
so pure bright we dare
not meet its gaze,
so dove white its

incandescence
shames the sky. We bite
instead into the mundane, the
merely knowable, the things
which can be measured, named.

We plant, we harvest, labor
in birthing spasms, remake
all we can touch in our own
image. We become small, winged,
a blue skimmer across

the fluid eye of world, pinned by
archangel's sword—but were we coming
or going? Inhaling or exhaling?
We set up our instruments,
take a reading, note we are

off the charts. We sneak another
peek for the forbidden, find none,
the arbor in which we once nested
incinerated by the descent
of what might have been us.

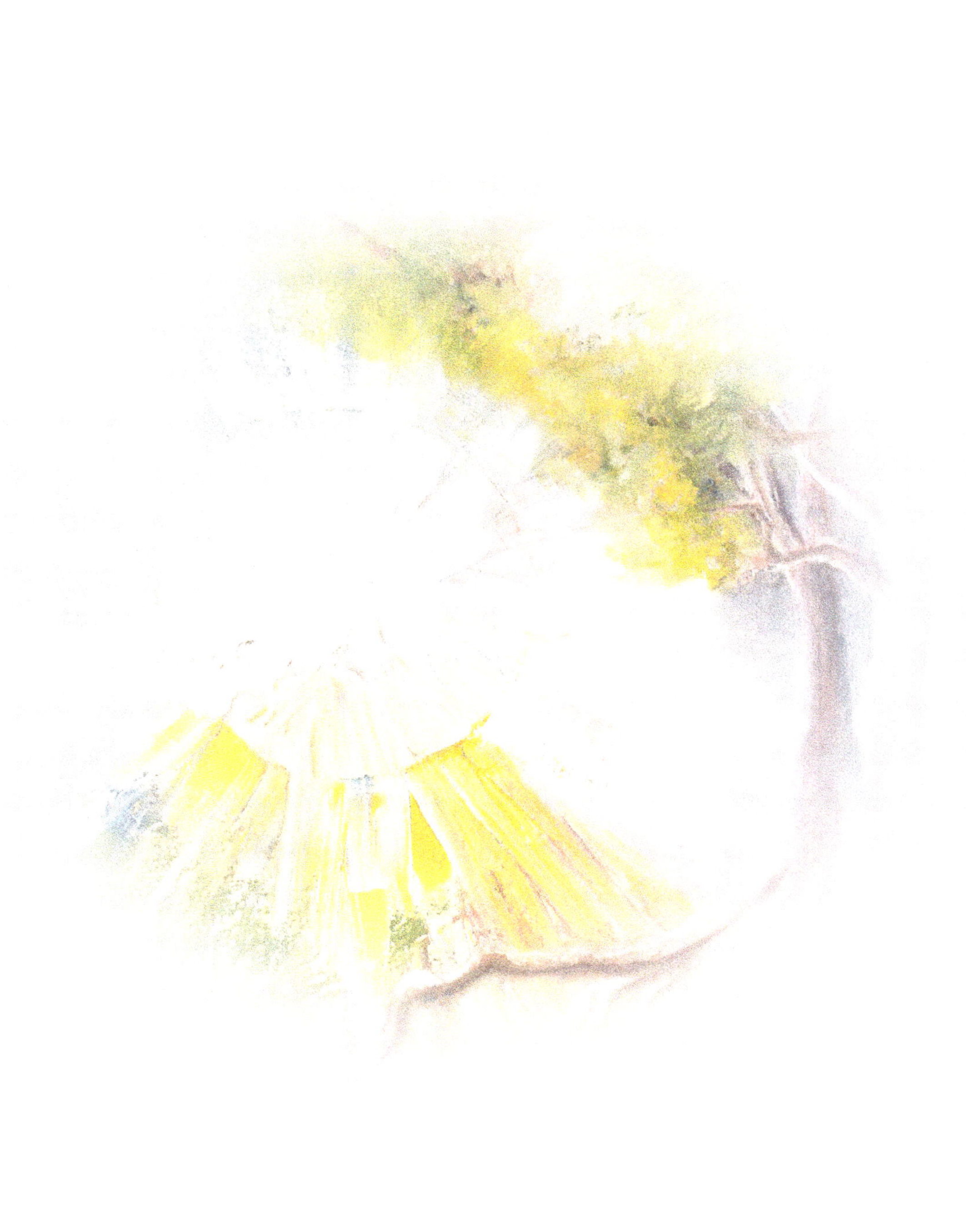

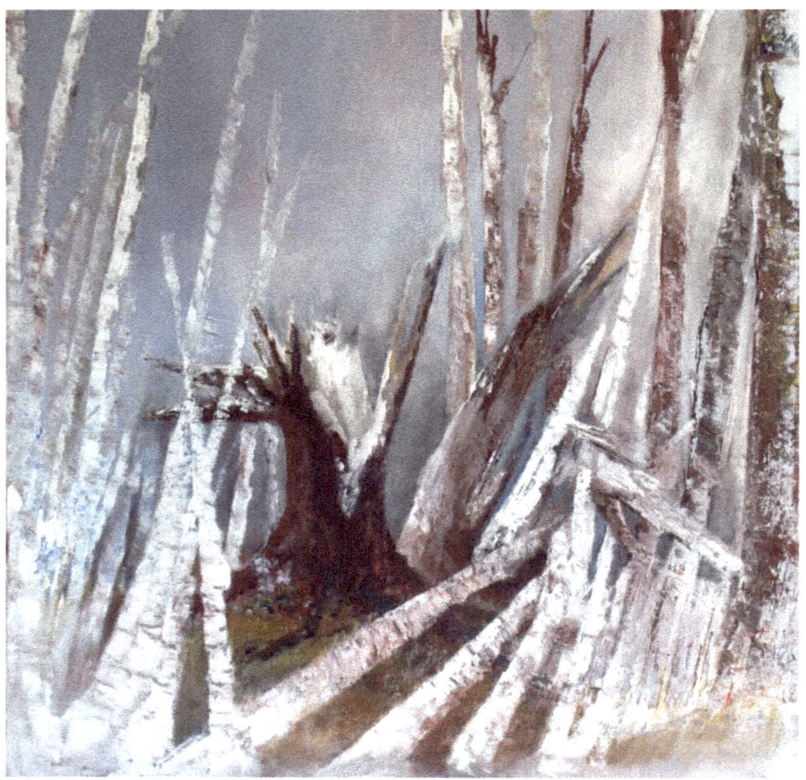

when i see birches

What Fire Feels Like

Splintered, split, his
beating heart speaks
tells tales of knowledge

good and evil, the
two legged-beings
who once walked

here, partook of his
fruit, though he
warned them, yes

he warned them
his eloquence
equal to the being

who slithered, but
he had no promises
to offer, no fork-

tongued whispers
of life amongst the gods
oh children, my children

but the birches
know nothing of
conflagration, pestilence

the quick wrath
of the finger of God
they have birthed

from the ashes
the distant smoky sky
their father

destined to die young
they offer him
nothing

for all his wisdom
tales of heat and love
and loss, what angels' wings

sound like, the mighty utterances
of creation, the gnashing
of teeth, the taste

of the sweat of the brow
they will never know
fire, will never survive it

when it strikes again
listen, now, the slither
comes

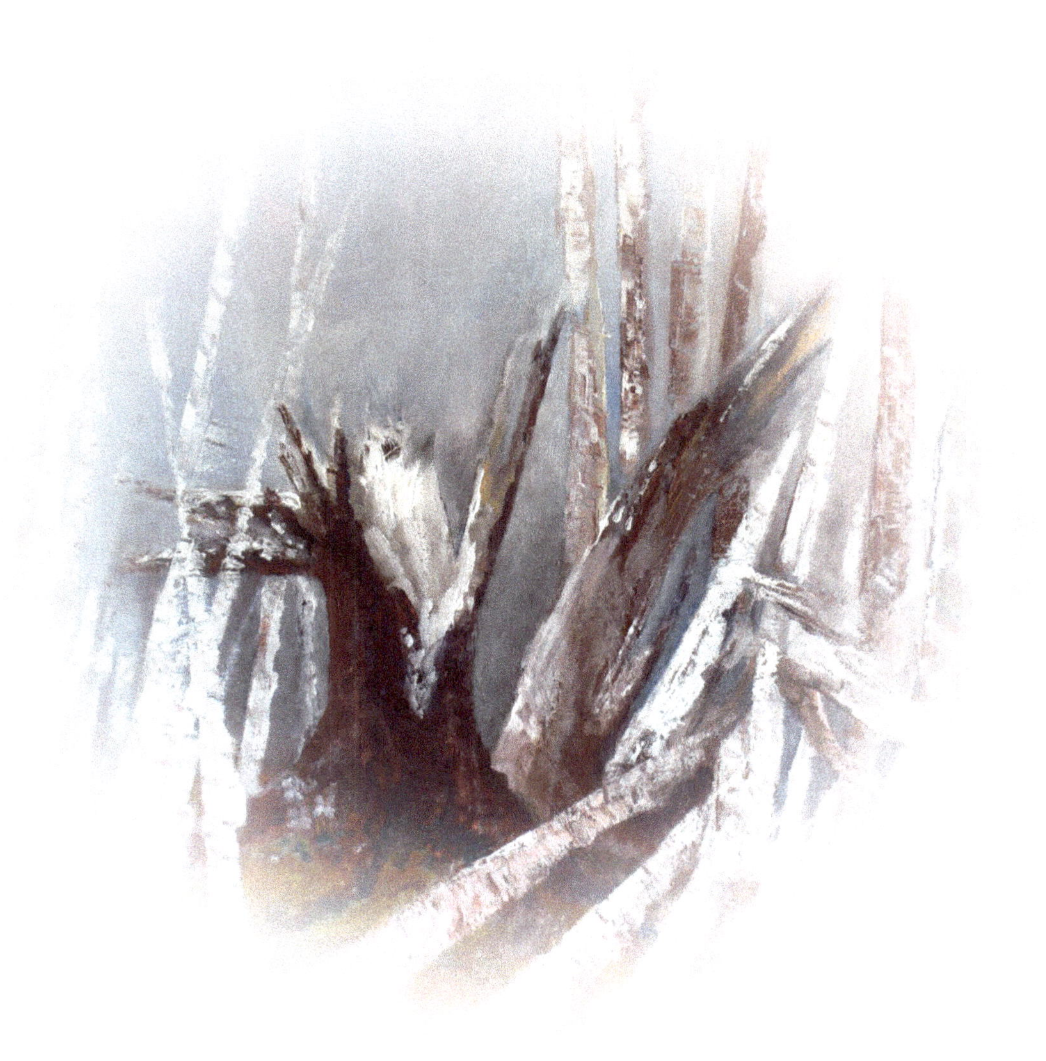

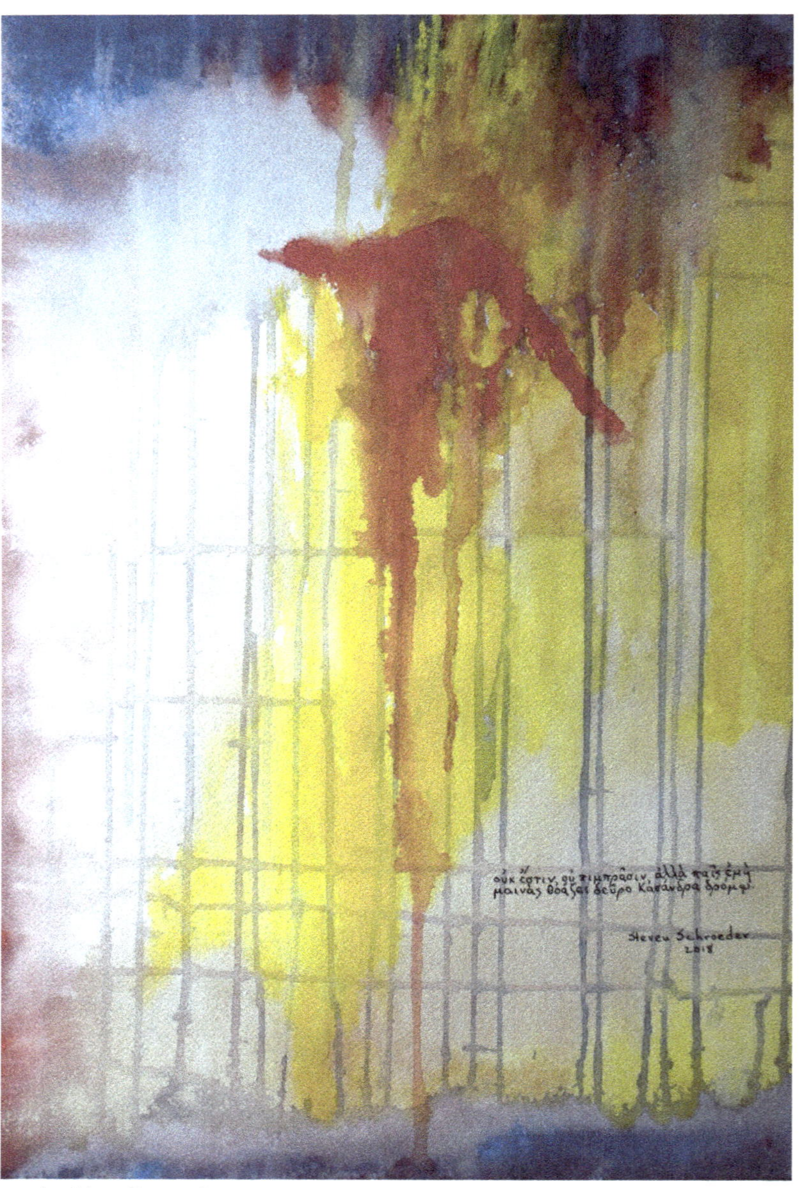

a gift of fire: Cassandra

In the Time of Falling Fire

Do we see this coming? Do we
keep our asbestos souls close at hand,
ready to unfurl in the brimstone rain?

Or are the sockets of our second sight
parched with plague and prophecy,
plunder and pillage, the ways of

this world? Are we doomed to
disbelieve our own oracles,
fail to fire the hollow horse

we both accept and hide
within? And when the walls fall,
are we the victors or the

vanquished? Is it not ourselves
we rape as we cling to
the owl-eyed patron

of Heracles and Perseus, sprung
fully formed from our own
Olympian foreheads? Are we

seer enough to see the end
when we call it down upon
us, our blood boiling

in the melting sky, scalding a river back
to the source? Or will we be hero enough
to behead the viperous reflection

so familiar in our shields
before this summer, endless,
arrives? Hero enough, perhaps,

to save a world?

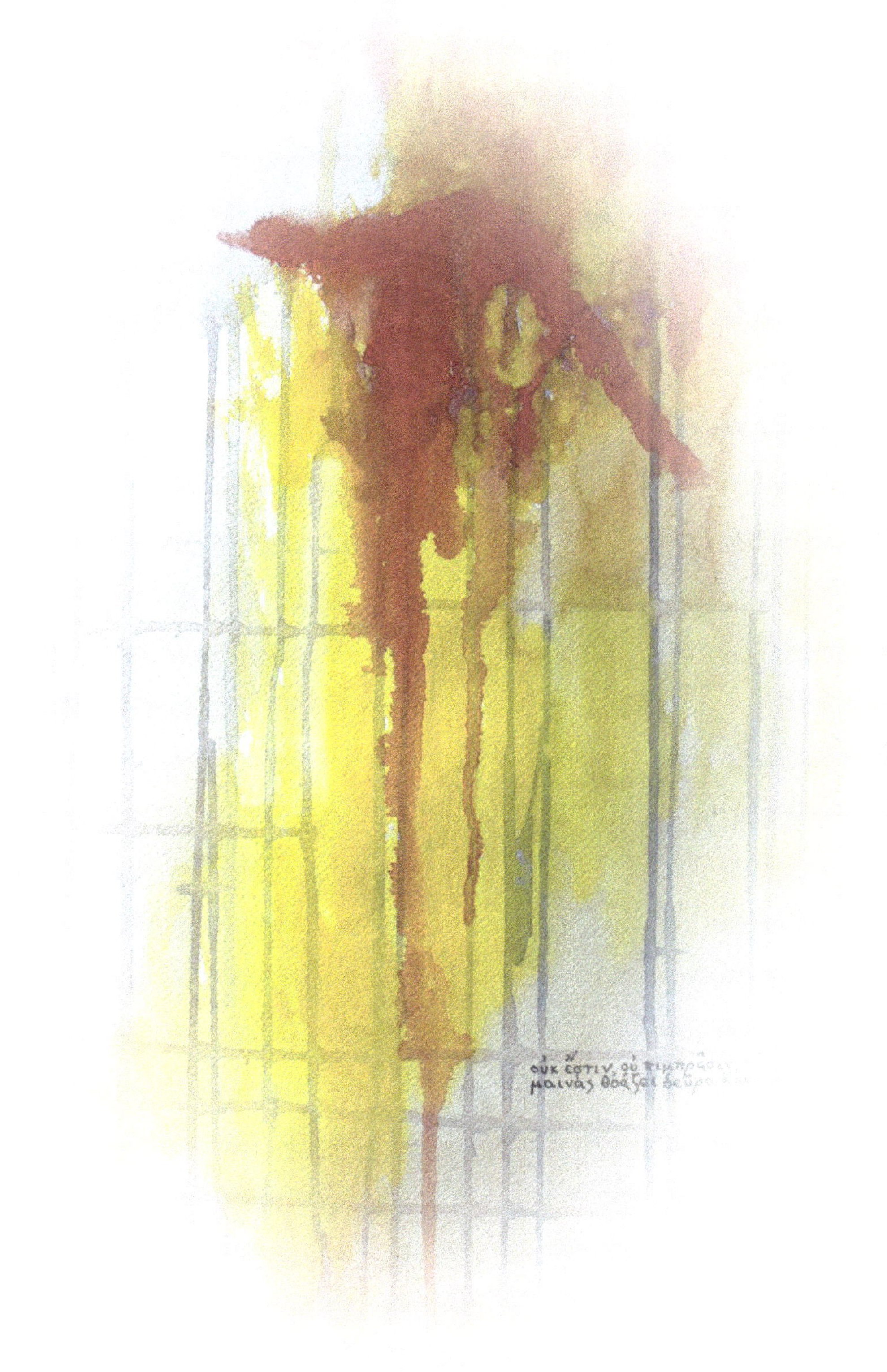
οὐκ ἔστιν οὖ τιμωρός
μαίνας θοάζει δεῦρο

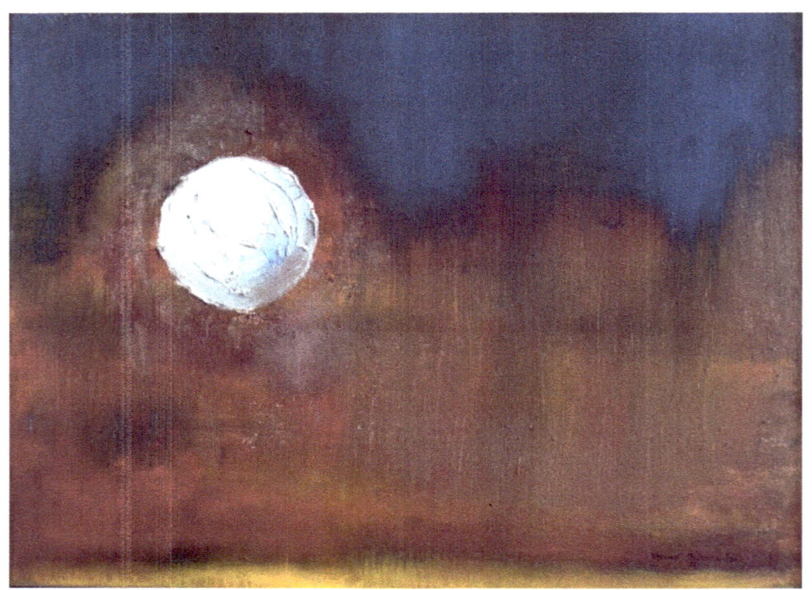

long night moon

Trinity

Atomic rain patters like the fingers of God on the glass of the phone booth. I dial zero for the operator, ask the area code for the moon. She says *One moment, please,* then comes back and says *I'm sorry, that number is no longer in service.* I ask *What number? I only asked for the area code.* She says, *The moon has been disconnected.*

Don't give me that crap, I say, looking out at the vermillion sky. *I can see it, big as a baseball right before it smacks you in the face.* A pause. *What number are you calling from?* she asks, and I read her the number from the white paper in the center of the dial, and she tells me that number's been disconnected. *That's impossible,* I tell her. *I'm talking to you, aren't I?* and she's got her comeback ready, she's been waiting for it: *I don't know. Are you?*

It's 5:35 AM and the white desert sand has melted to glowing green glass, and I'm not in the mood to play games. *Okay,* I say. *If you can't get me the moon, get me the future.* Some clicking on the line, then: *Please deposit one cent.*

That's all? I ask. *One cent for the future?*

The future isn't what it used to be. Nasdaq crashed six minutes ago.

Six minutes. 5:29 AM. The Gadget. The mushroom cloud. Forty seconds later, the shock wave. In three weeks, Little Boy, Fat Man. Seven years, Ivy Mike. Nine, Castle Bravo. Seventeen, Cuba. I don't know from Nasdaq, but it can't be good.

I deposit a penny. Four rings later a man's voice says: *The Future can't come to the phone right now. Please leave a message after the tone.* Then nothing. The voice sounds a lot like mine, the nothing a lot like what I'd dreaded. I say nothing, leave the void a void. I'm getting ready to hang up, to cry, to put my fist through the glass, when the operator comes back on: *Sir?* She has to repeat it several times. *Yes?* I say, finally. *I'm curious,* she says. *About why you asked for the moon.*

Because, I say. *In no time at all, we'll be up there. I wanted to warn somebody. The Man in the Moon, I wanted him to know. 'Now I am become Death, the destroyer of worlds.'*

I'm so sorry, Dr. Oppen___er. The line is breaking up. *Please return_____bunker. You wouldn't want them______ome and find you___ing to ___self___* And I am left holding only the red-hot night in my hand.

From the bunker, *Moonlight Sonata* whispers, Teller at his Steinway. The first movement so tranquil. I can only imagine how he'll thunder when he gets to the third.

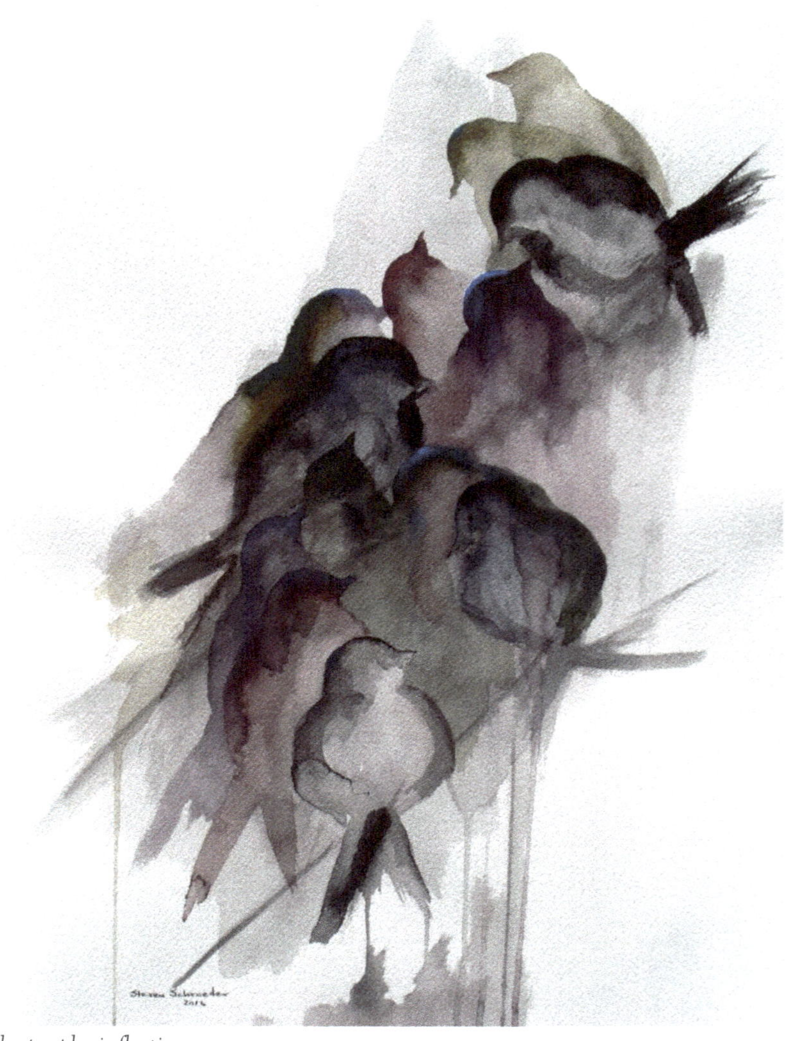

sky people: inflections

Birds on a Wire

We negotiate for balance
smudges of our former selves

chattering in air that isn't
what it used to be

clinging to pathways
our voices no longer

travel, wondering
how much farther

we can wing it
before our conclave is

burnt

drowned

smothered

blown to bits

separated at the border

of the conscious
and the nothing

always just beyond us
used to be something

worth dying for
we die in a void now

how did that happen
whose side are we on

is there more than
one side anymore

there are a million
ways to migrate

it seems and none of them
leads us home

back to the nest
where last we felt

safe
feathers unruffled

the birthing sun
burnished by the

sweet

dewy

breath

of a new day

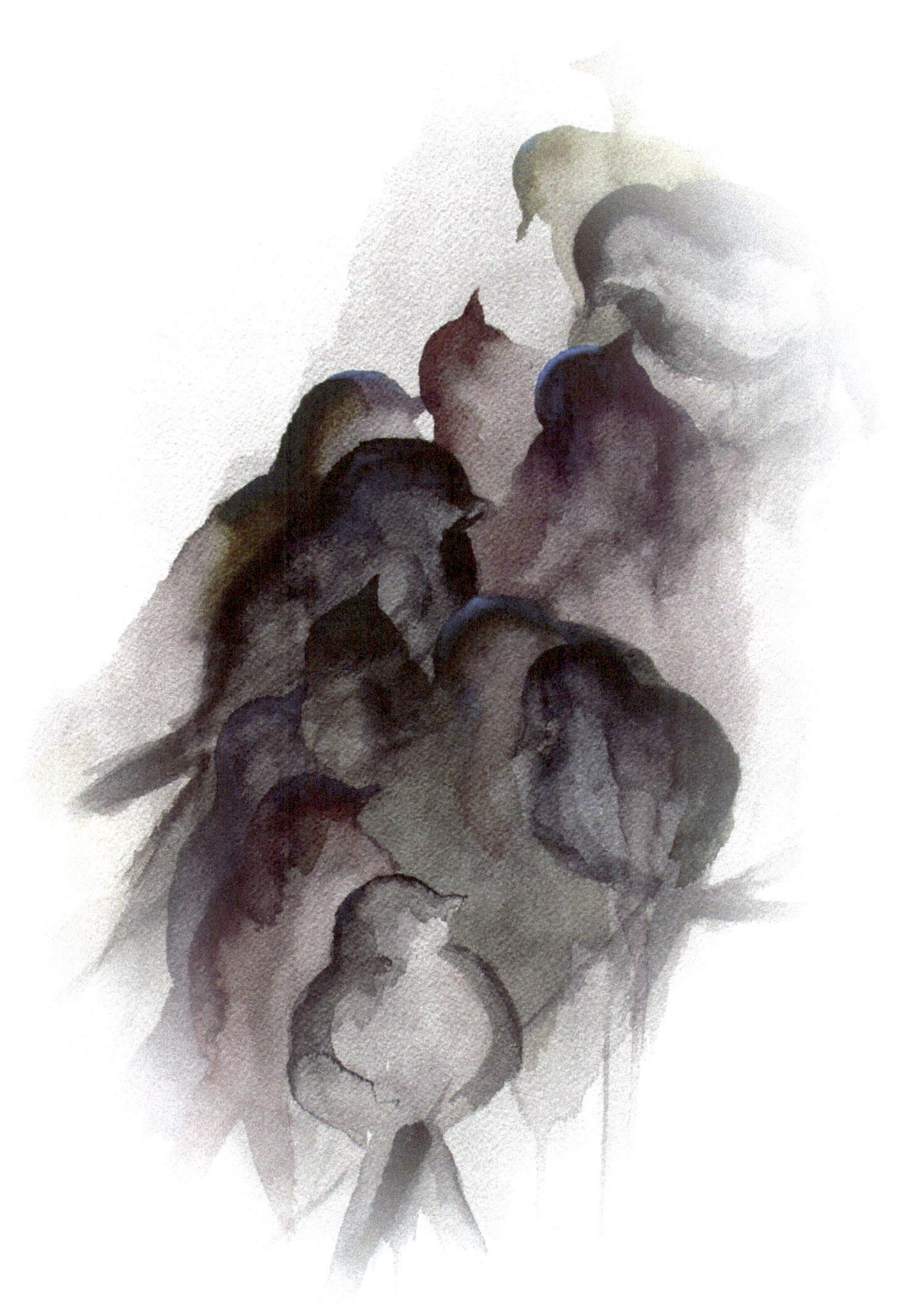

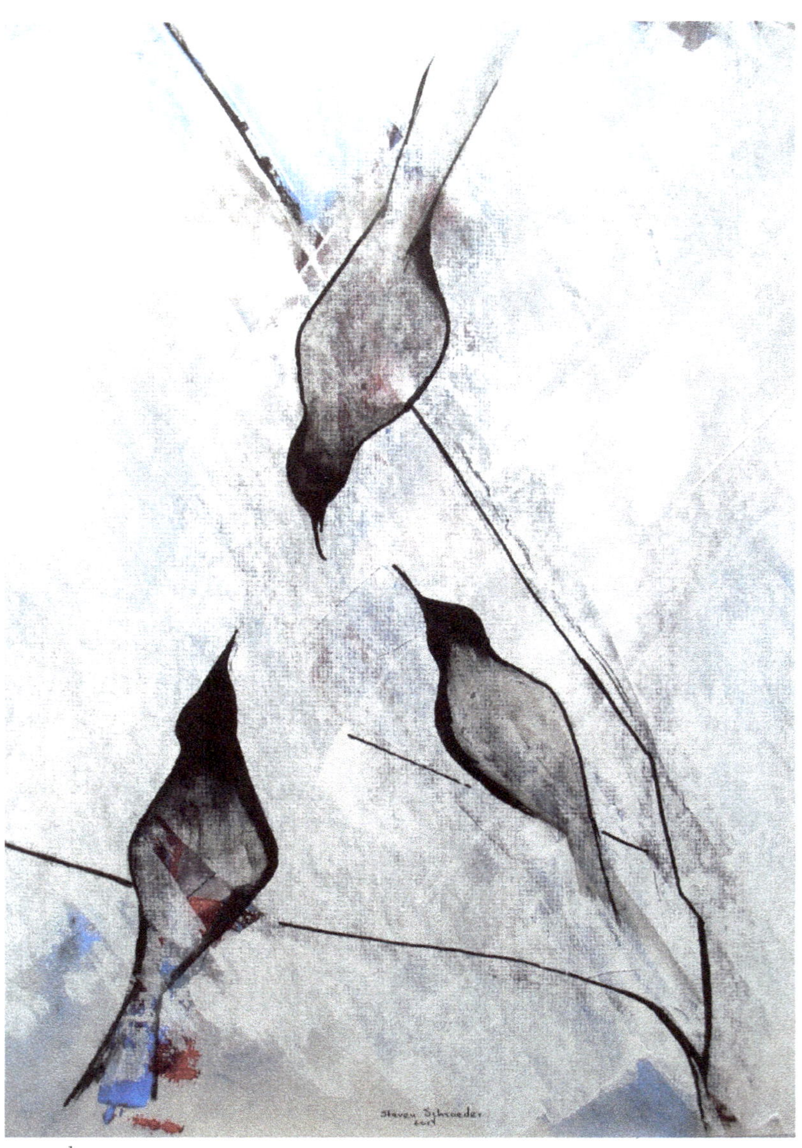

a murder

Roadkill

A knife to the gut, a bullet
center body mass, the smashing pumpkin
sound of a pool cue to the head,

that's all they ask. A hit
and run, a garotte chewing into
flesh, a few too many

sleeping pills. A war
would be nice: Korea, Iran,
Venezuela, they're not picky,

they travel light. A bloated child
or two on the trail up from Honduras.
A Lopez or Ramirez-Marcano

unresponsive on cold Big Spring
TX cement. In a Newark alley,
the spilled-coffee sprawl

of a junkie's last fix. A school,
any school, any active shooter
situation anywhere. The menu's

a blank slate and their minds' eyes
always bigger than their gizzards.
They never forget a face, especially one

with lids wide open, staring up at
the infinite. A little famine
now and then, perhaps, to tide them

over. And don't get them started
on fire, flood, and pestilence. Global warming,
they're up for it, up to a point—bodies corrupt

quicker in the heat. But extinction,
no thank you. Dead planet, the only
corpse that's no use to them.

One murder too many.

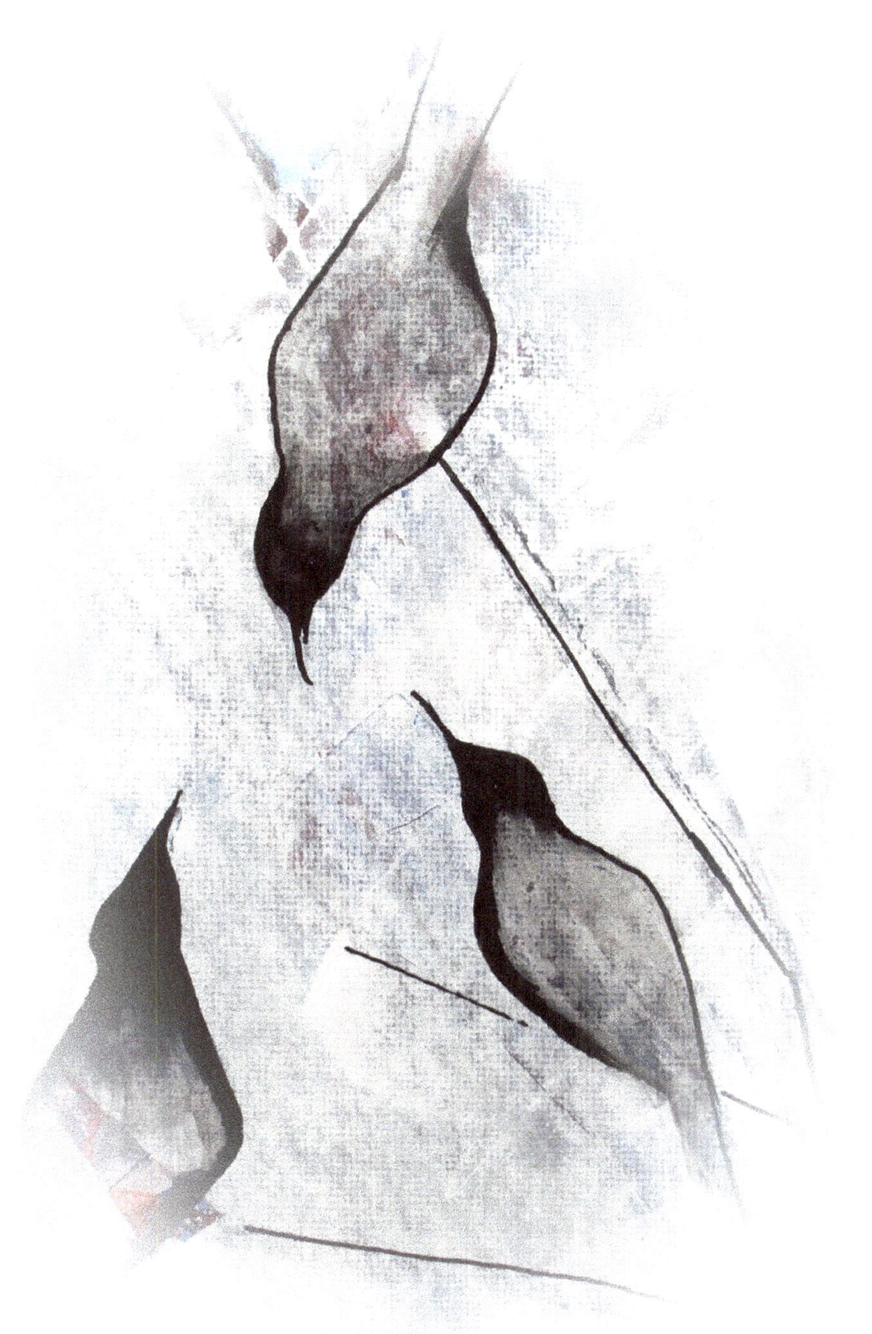

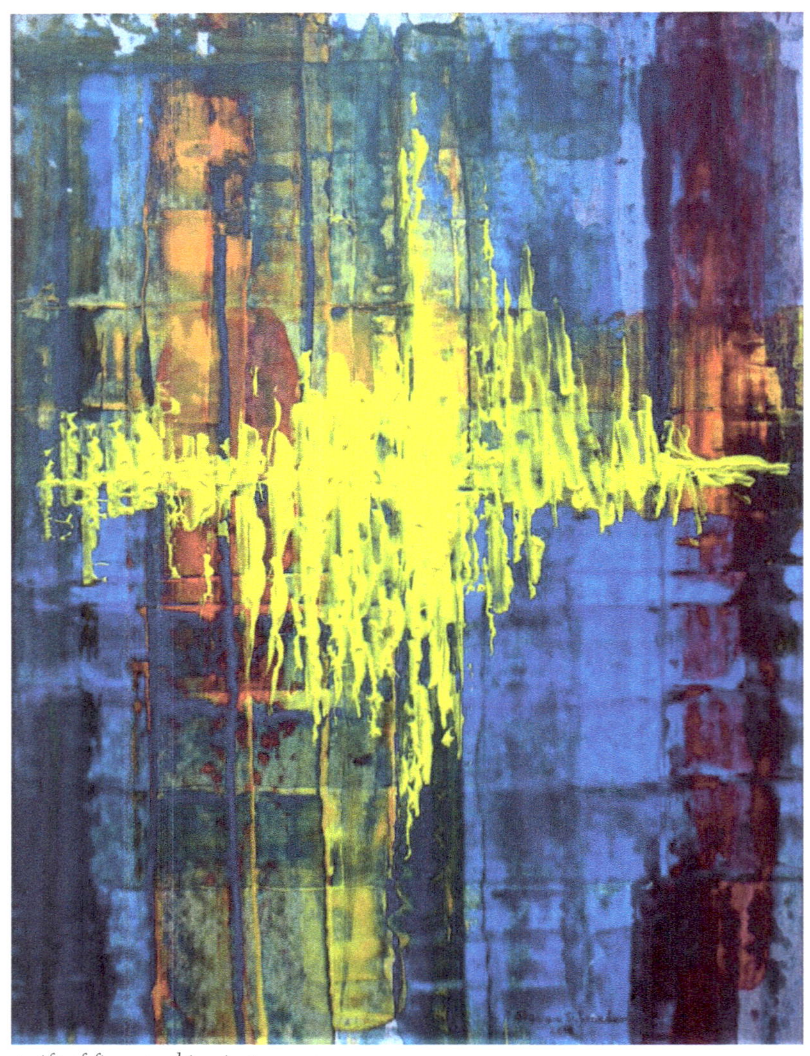

a gift of fire: speaking in tongues

What is the Frequency, Kenneth?

We fiddle with the tuner knobs of our brains,
touch-drag the scrolling iPhone screens

of our hearts, and still we can't find it. We tap
the probes of our inner oscilloscopes, tinker with

psychogenic sonar transponders, try to sound the depths
of souls in passing, the fathoms of the unfamiliar.

Primary colors dance across the cones
of our retinas, yet our circadian rhythms

are out of step, our clocks chime only discord.
We bombard each other with subatomic particles

of hate, jealousy, greed, colors not on
the wheel of good fortune, wonder why

the system fails us, create straw men,
lie in wait for them on the darkened streets

of our inner selves, are surprised when
our victims turn out to be our attackers,

when the Kenneth we believe responsible
for it all looks like us in a mirror,

and still we do not know the frequency,
cannot find the common ground,

ford the stream, bridge the chasm,
calm the tremblors along the fault lines

of ourselves. And so, we repeat the question
ad infinitum, shout it from the rooftops,

while standing in the gutters of our lives,
fingers in our ears, refusing to believe that

Kenneth is the frequency.

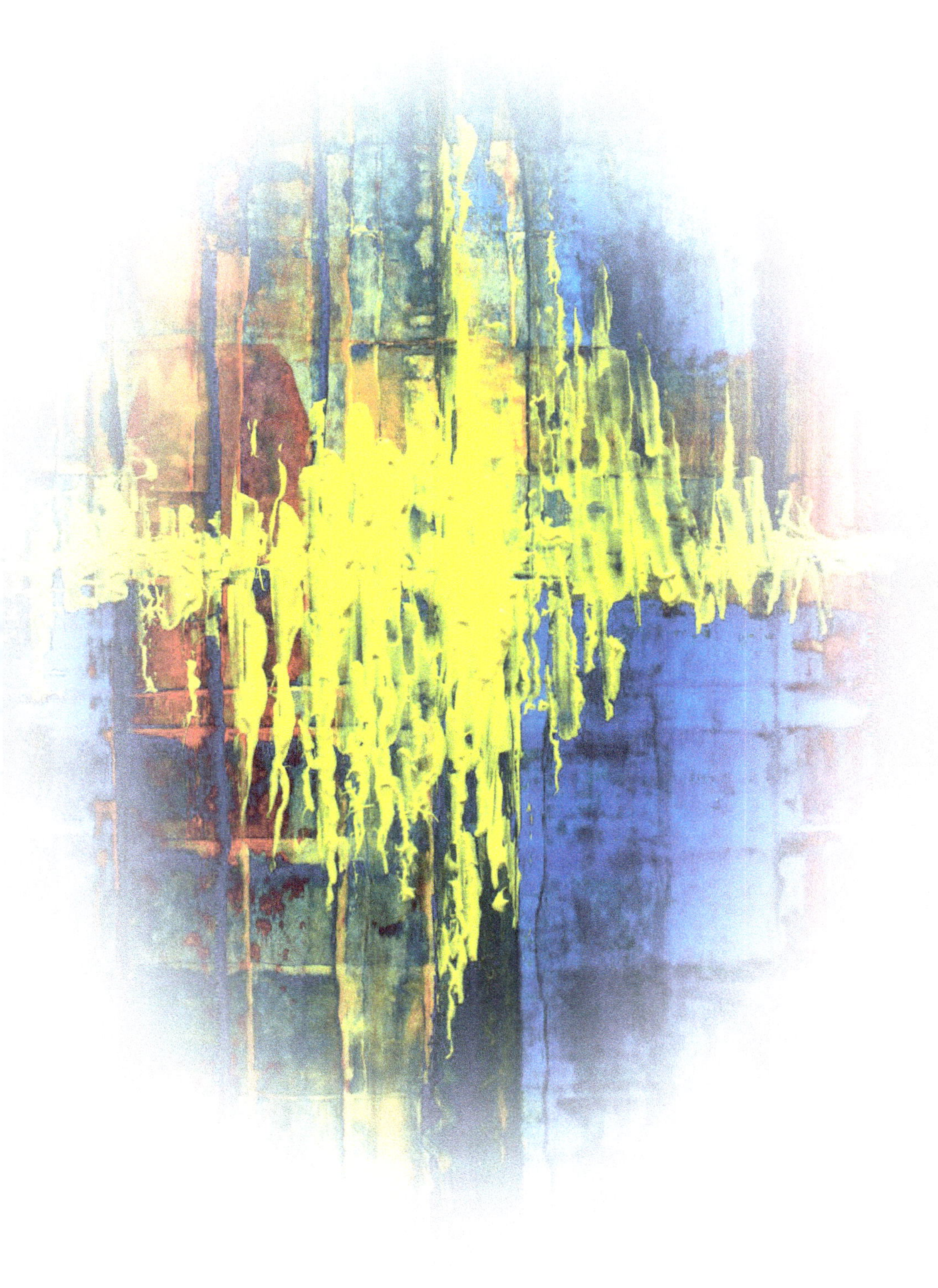

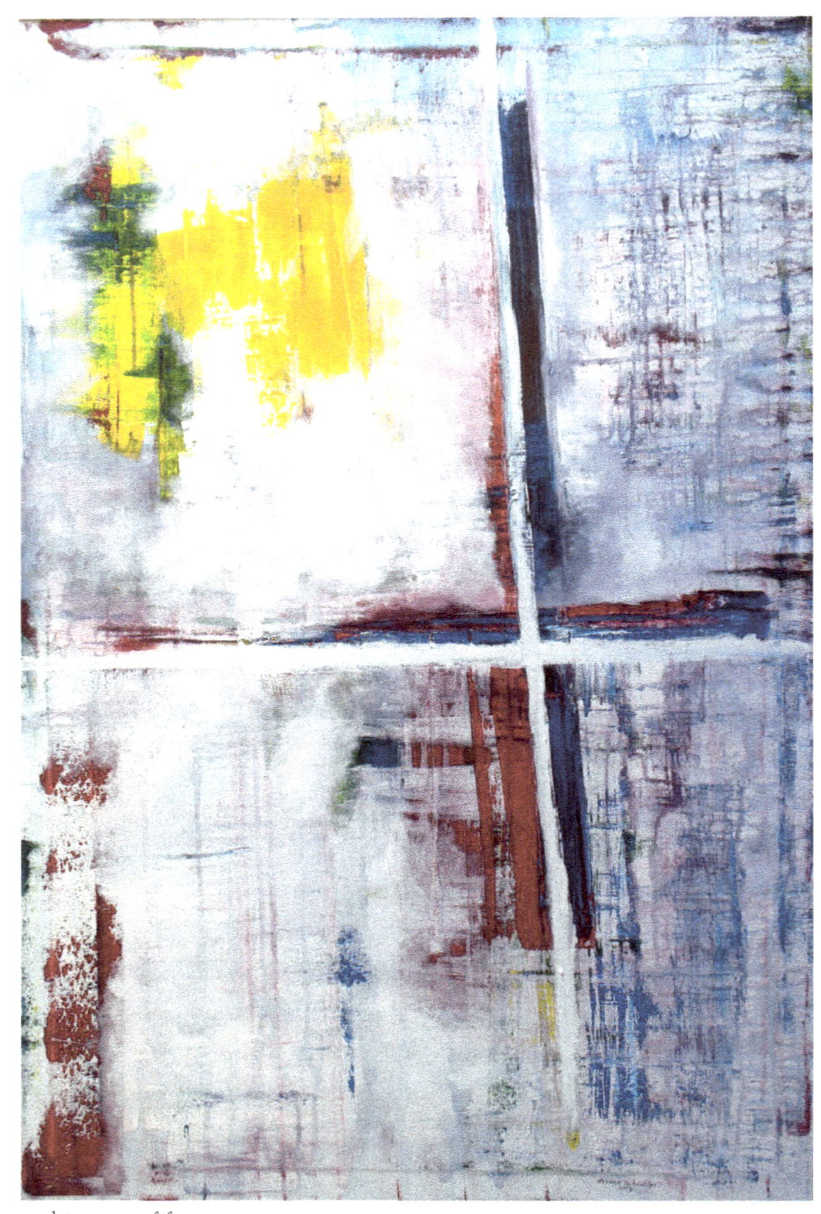

architecture of fear

The Watcher

He is out there. She. It. Them. Looking in.
Thinks he's/they're hiding in the lower right
quadrant, deep blue sea. I see (anyway) the face
(looking) in (we see). Torches blaze caution in white fog
(night/s?). Blood-hungry crocodile slithers left pane
to right, eyeing me/us from beneath blue fishhooks,
fleshless bait I/we do (not) (yet) take. Do not
(I/we do not) understand the croc, do not (I/we)
comprehend the why of (this)
watching, you/she/it/them flaming
advertisement (one) moment, Davey
Jones locker (the next). I (We?) have nothing
you/it/they want(s). Have done
nothing (wantable). Am (not I) guiltless.
Am not (I) watching the watcher. Watch
me. Who is watching (me/us). (Who) is me/us
watching. Everything turned (in)side(out)ways.
Clues (what we/they look for/need) (will) reveal.
Lower left quadrant, (the) blood (about
to be spilled) smudges the glass. Mine
(maybe). Yours (maybe). Theirs (definitely,
whoever they are/all of us/maybe). In this
together, we are (not). Out of this (together)
we are not. We are (not). We fear (naught, and
always and everything). We are (you are/I am) out (of this) there.
Looking (in). What do we/they see (ourselves/themselves)
in the act of committing/omitting. Shiver me timbers (cold/sudden).
Spy who (didn't) come in from. Eye/I turn up
trench coat collar, turn down I/eye patch,
blend (don't) into (absent) shadows, entangle
us (me) in hooks, rend flesh (the croc rends flesh—
do we/I/us/he/she/it/them understand now?),
a leg/arm here/there, scattered (the pieces

of me/you, what I/we/everyone feared),
diamond screams cutting through
(the) glass in (side) out. (Can) we stitch
us/bodies/world (back) together. (What a)
Frankenstein we (will) make.

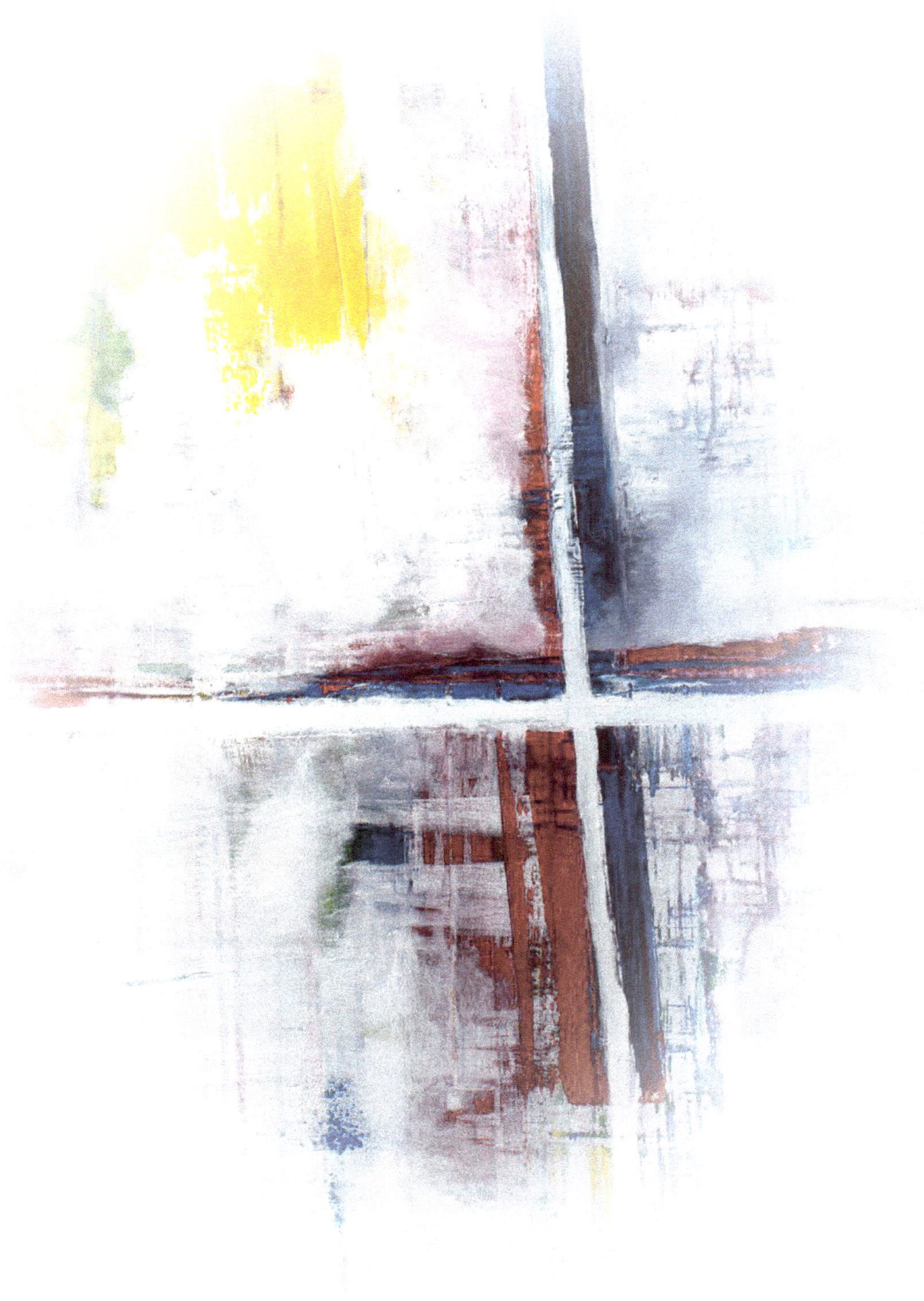

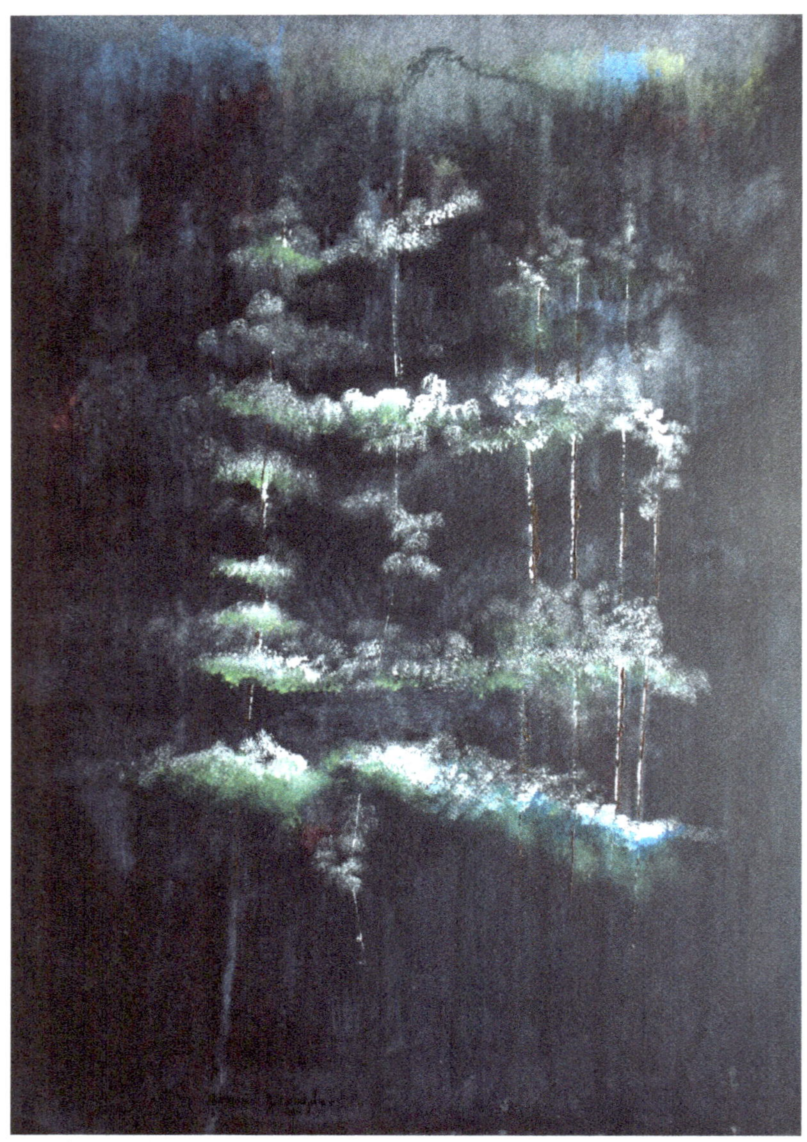

event horizon 2

The One the Brothers Grimm Left Out

This is the cathedral of the collapsed world,
the sanctuary of hopes abandoned, the museum of
emotional discombobulation, the point

of no return at the end of the line
of futility. The trees in this forest
of eternal night are shades of fairy tales,

extruding ectoplasmic evergreen fingers
misconceived in the absence
of photosynthesis, the absence of you, of any

bright beating heart. This timber roots
in the topsoil of desolation, the cinders
of burned-at-the-stake love. The hoot of the owl

of despair echoes nonstop,
the bay of the wolf of eternal winter,
the wasted beauty of the nightingale's aria.

O, I was born here, as I've come to believe,
birthed into eternal abandonment, emerging
now and then at the whisper

of footsteps such as yours, walking
with you a bit down the road
until we come to that hostel

known as the Parting of the Ways,
at which there is no bed with my name,
no space for me at the table,

not even the ghost of a wave
from you as you enter, the dawn a rumor
on the horizon, breadcrumbs

which I have strewn, needlessly,
on the road back to the land
of wicked stepmothers, poisoned

apples, children served up for
dinner, the country where happy endings
go to die, where I consume the gruel

of grief, the stones of self-pity, croak
my kiss-shunned frog prince lullaby
deep and deep and deep into the night.

Part Three

Escape Velocity

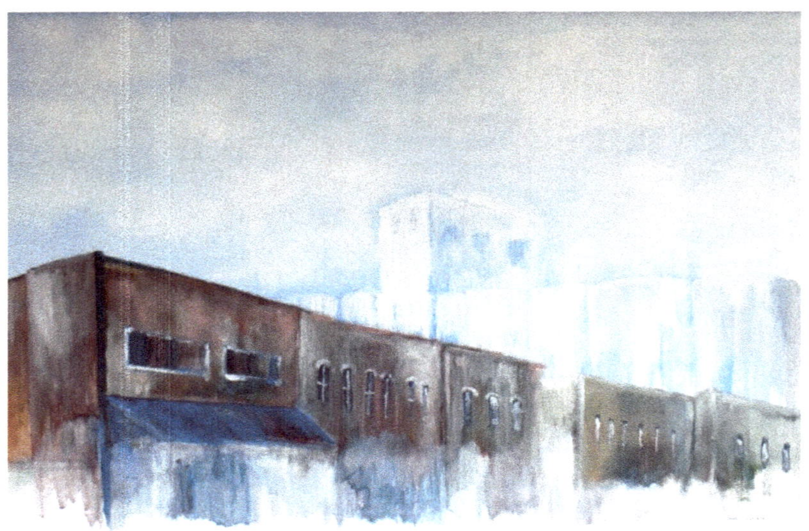

politics

Ghost Town

Once, we all lived here.

Those white figures waving from the
windows, they're what we left behind.
And those crosses, they mark those of us

who jumped. The first floors, the retail shops
where we sold our souls to the highest bidder,
they are memory erasing from the ground

up. Even the Van Gogh blue of the awning
over the sidewalk café where we used to gather
for coffee and miracles

rains absence. No wonder we feel
unfinished, spectres of our former selves.
And that looming, hulking, half-seen thing

merging with or emerging from
the once-upon-a-time Côte d'Azur
sky, that is us tomorrow, looking over

our vanishing shoulders,
hording kernels
of what might have been.

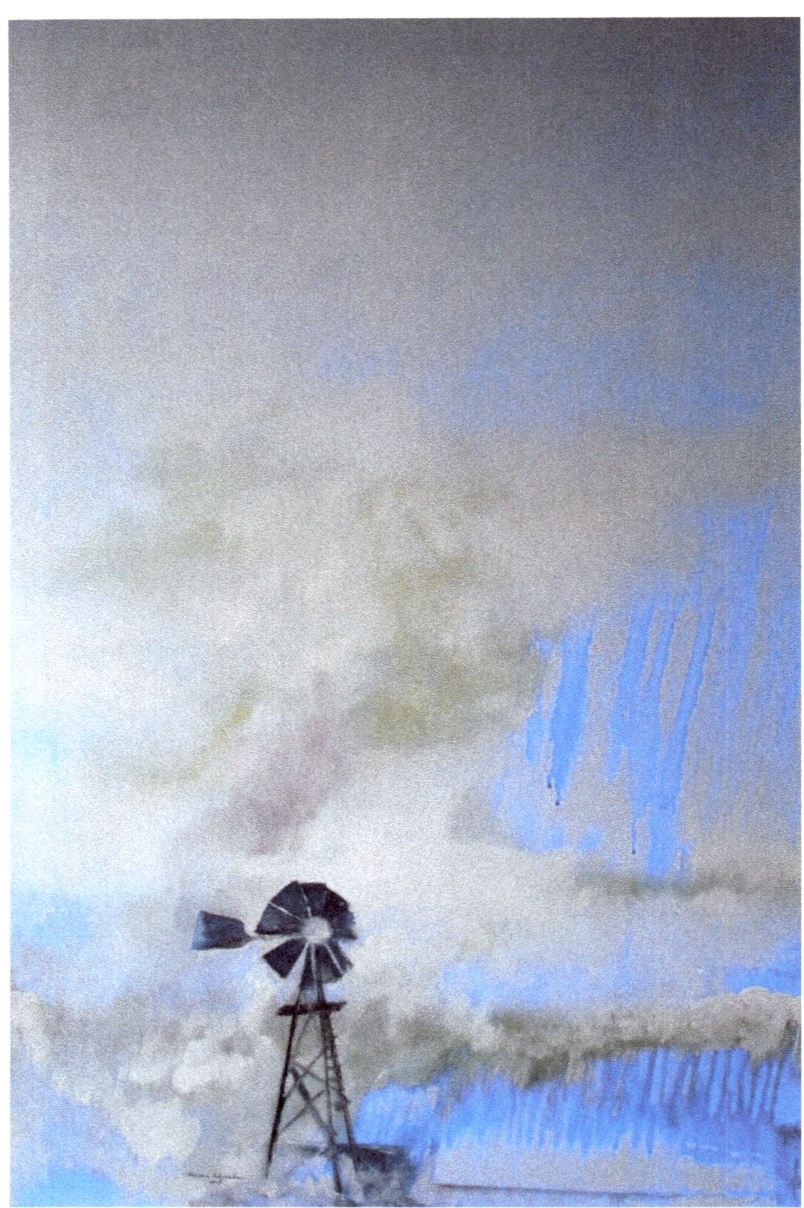

nothing makes it work

Windmill

You see it
on the side of the graveled road
traveling north from Highway 4
towards the bones
of a town called Hope

you know it
or believe you do
the wind passing its blessing hand
over the spikey red-brown heads
your grandfather used to call

hard red winter
and you thought at first
he was talking about
a season
only later you figured out he meant

his life
your life
all the lives
of all the people he fed
all of the hard red winter people everywhere

and you feel his hand
the ghost of it
passing over your Brylcreemed
crew cut
the red-brown spikes of it

the hard rubber ridges
of a tire as tall as you
cutting into the seat of your Lee jeans
the chug of the John Deere's four cylinders
pumping air with a rhythm you will only later

associate with the perpetuation of life
the sowing of the next generation
only today in fact
just you in the Hyundai
and the ghost of callous-handed hope

and you wonder who owns it now
when the roof fell in
the barn collapsed
what made you drive up here this particular day
after all the leavings

lawyers
fingers not touching
lips not opening except to hurl
hard red winter words
what do you expect to find here

the summer of your youth
is long gone
it walked out the door with Ruth and Emily and Bobby
you turn on the wipers
as the sky begins to cry

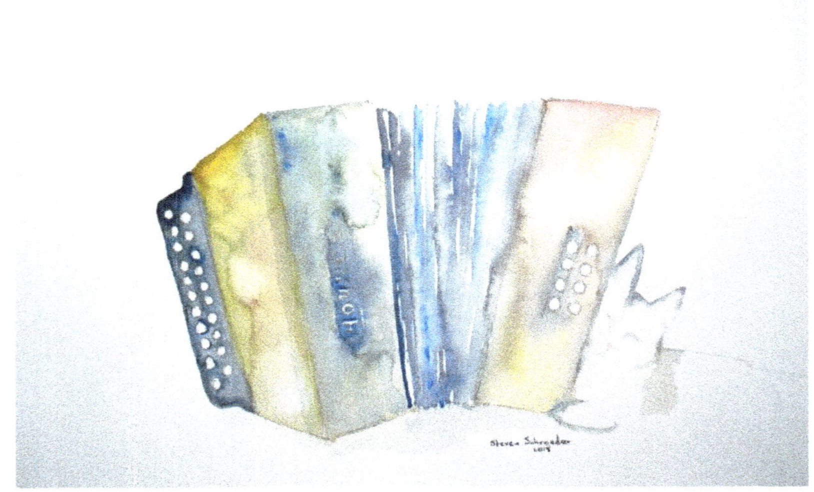

Grandpa's ghost

Squeezebox

Grandpa never played the accordion, or any other instrument, for that matter, unless you count the blues harp I coveted as a kid, settled in for the long haul next to the circular pipe rack full of calabashes, corn cobs, briars, beechwoods, the odd meerschaum and cavalier, none of which ever appeared anywhere other than in their locked and loaded stand-at-attention stations between the harmonica and two greasy, clipped-eared packs of Bicycle playing cards held together with rotting rubber bands, all of which, together with a couple of dented bowling trophies and a slightly rusted metal plaque that read *God watches over Drunks, Old Ladies, Little Children, and The International Association of Machinists*, cluttered up the only shelf in what Grandpa referred to as his "den," but which was actually a converted breakfast nook. Clues, perhaps, to some pre-grandpa grandpa I never knew.

So why this apparition appears to me now, rattles and wheezes its way through my long, restless nights, I don't know. Perhaps the worn-beyond-reading lettering, which could be Hohner, the same brand on the blues harp, or could be just nothing at all, a figment of my imagination, is a clue? And how do I know this ghost is Grandpa?

The cat, all pale and purring-eyed, snuggled up to the left-hand button box. Priss. Stella's cat. Stella, the second of Grandpa's four wives. Priss, who always rubbed up against me whenever Mom wore Dad down enough to shame him into taking the lot of us over to see his own father. Priss, whose solution to many long gaps in conversation was to rub my leg, my brother's leg, Dad's leg, Mom's, the magazine rack with last week's newspaper in it, the second-hand-store floor lamp. Priss, who cat-napped with her head on Grandpa's shoe, sock, slipper, whatever happened to be the fashion of the day.

Until Stella kicked Grandpa out, for reasons never made clear to two not-quite teenaged boys.

But today, this Saturday morning, when, for the last time, I get out of the bed you and I once shared, the Stones' *Back Street Girl* waltzing on the squeezebox of my mind, Ginger the cat batting at my brown wingtip shoestrings; when I peer in at the still sleeping boys, wonder what kind of nightmares they will make of it; when I pass the shelf in the family room full of sea shells and driftwood collected before my time, take up the scratched and tarnished Hohner from its place in the midst of the pre-us of us and slip it into the pocket of my silk shirt, feel the cold of it against my heart; when I go out our mortgaged front door once and for all, harsh words from last night haunting my wake; when I steer the Beemer towards Suzie's place, plotting what day to come back for the rest of my things—maybe, just maybe, I understand.

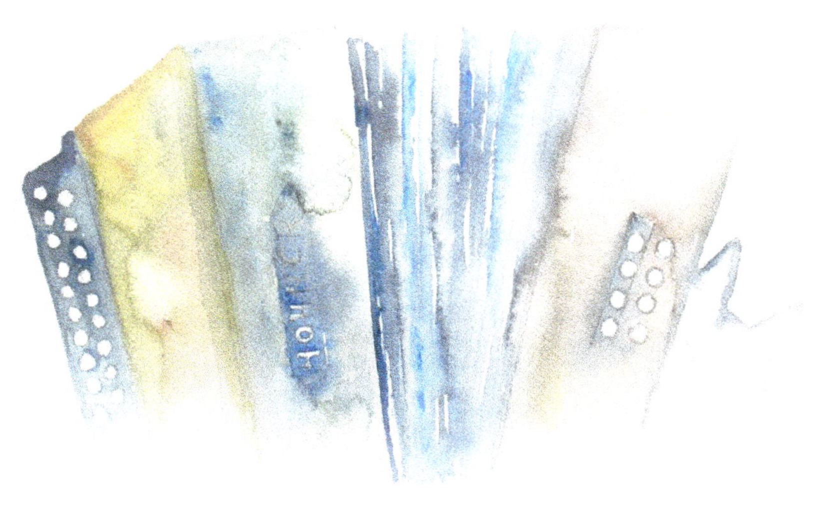

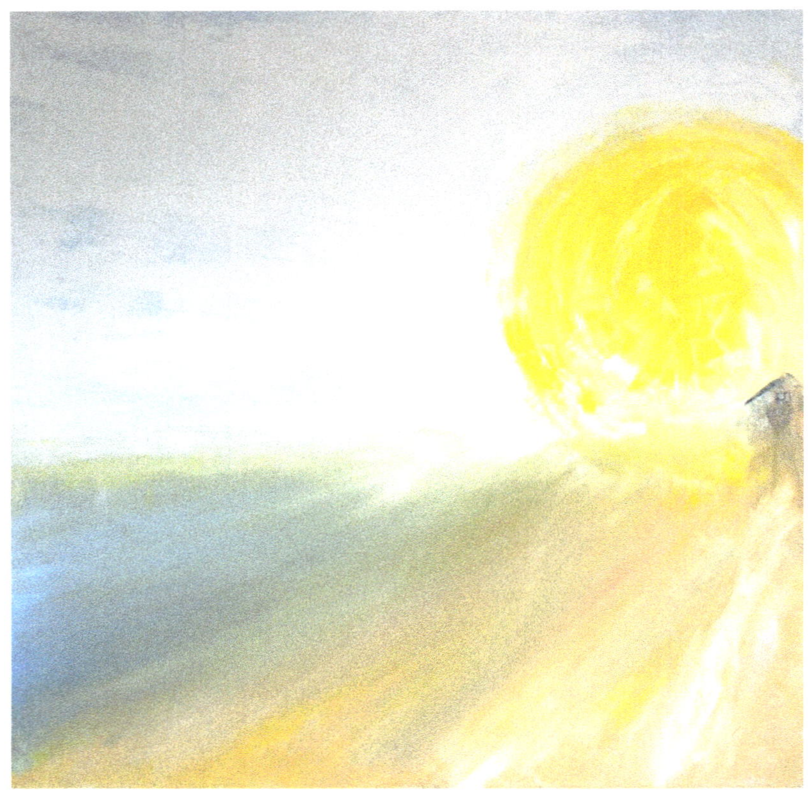

all that is solid melts into air

What I Remember

What I remember is the sun, and how,
in those days, we all lived within

a stone's throw of it. What I remember
is my mother's clear-nailed fingers

clacking over the ivories of the
upright piano, and how the notes danced

in the warm green irises of her eyes. What I
remember is my father taking his father's

handmade board and whittled wood pegs
from the battered cigar box which, nevertheless,

was laden with wondrous treasure,
shuffling dogeared blue cards backed

with winged Cupid riding a bicycle,
and explaining words like cribbage

and his nibs, the difference between
play and show. What I remember

is the Sunday afternoon smell of pot roast
and string beans and scalloped potatoes

coming to a head in the butter-colored
sanctum sanctorum of the kitchen. What

I remember is tiny miles of railroad track
on a big brown board in the basement

and little brother's ecstatic hand claps
when the train left the rails. What I remember

is catch in the backyard, and how much Dad did
not resemble Catfish Hunter or Blue Moon Odom,

and how the light glinted off his fastball anyway.
What I remember is Miss Buttenhof's blonde hair,

and how we naughty little Lutheran School boys
never minded staying after hours in fourth grade.

What I remember is rounding the corner of the school
building and running into a new kid, and how,

when we got into our 40s & 50s, we faded out
of each other's lives. But mostly what I remember

is all the houses we ever lived in, and how they were
all the same house, because they were always our house.

If you look quickly, closely, you can see it now, our house,
just barely in frame, floating across the face of this

one last cigar-box-treasure day, me waving from the porch,
the sun still rising.

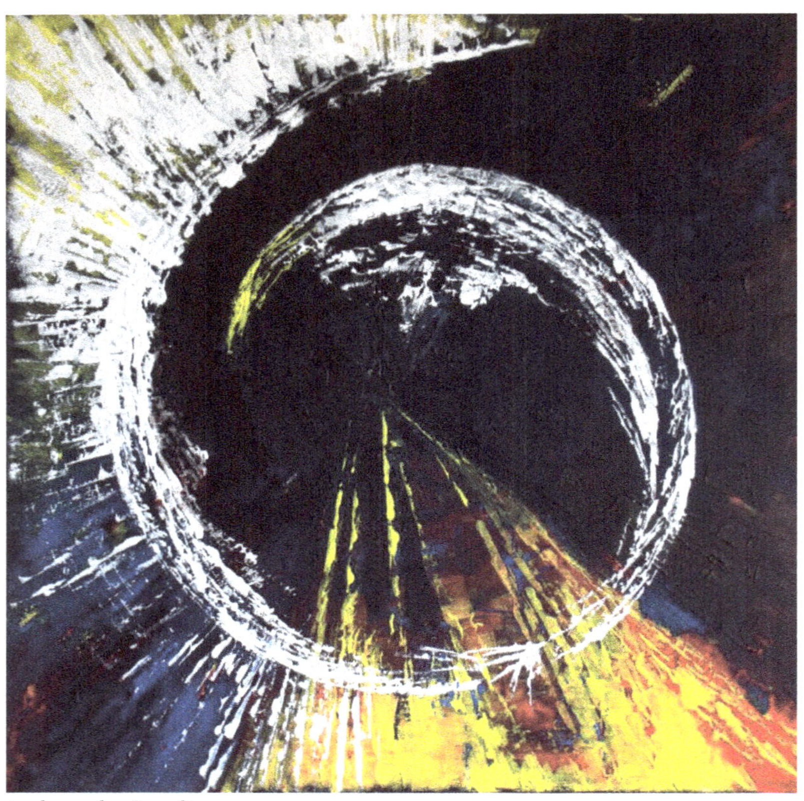

in the path of totality

Star Stuff

The summer of your sixth year
out of the clear blue sky
a gust of wind, the kite string

breaks, you can feel the loss
of it in your hands, the rolling
pin spool no longer unrolling,

the diamond you and Father
spent all weekend fashioning
from broomsticks and discarded

plastic drifting up and up
over fields and trees
and all the places

you've been and never will
be, up and up into the sun and
Kite Heaven is the answer

Father gives when you ask,
wet-cheeked, where kites go
when they die, and you

decide then and there
that when St. Peter meets you
at the gate you'll ask *Which way*

is Kite Heaven? and by Christmas
you have forgotten the kite, by
twenty you've forgotten heaven,

when your father dies you put away
all childish things, you buy your son
a PlayStation, a BMW, and now you

stare out the window of your
Senior Living bedroom
one blank moon summer night

and see only the absence
into which you will soon
descend, but look, look

there, raise up your head,
higher, higher still, that
blaze of glory rocketing

over the known
and the unknown, it's
a kite, all many-colored,

lighting a road
just for you, burnishing
the finger of the swirl of

star stuff you once called
God, now sleep, my little
one, sleep. Father is waiting.

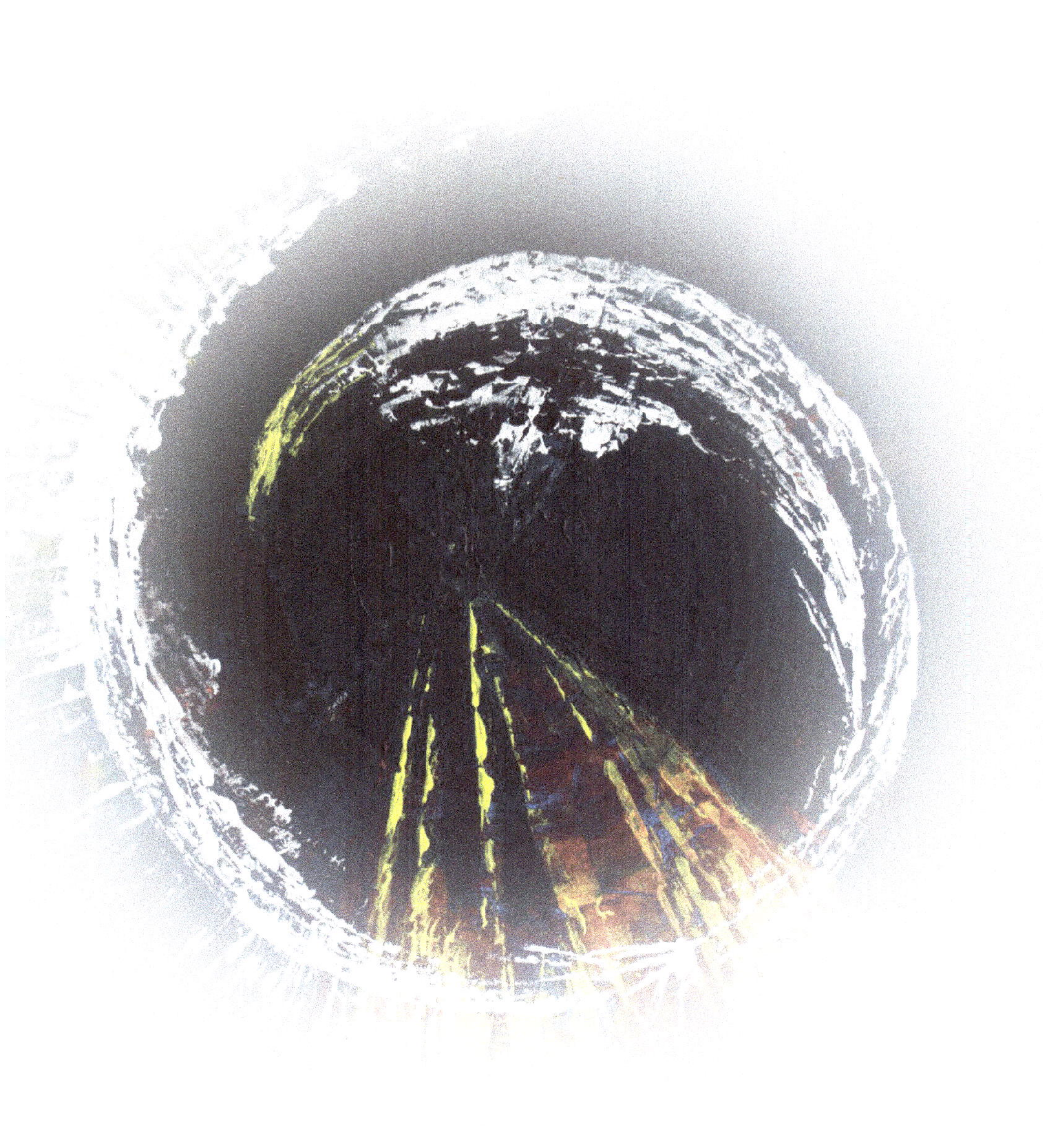

trouble the water

Trouble the Water

What do I see?
You. Me. Us.

A Bethesda of sorrows. The reflection
of an angel, reaching down.

That argument we had
last night, last week, last

year. The healing we strive for
today, blanket spread, the ichor

of day-old rain still embraced
by sweet green grass. Shall we

be made whole? Shall we take up
our bed and walk? The bread, the honey,

the wine, such fragrant miracles. Dare we
deny them their due? Dare we?

Shall we be less than the infirm
man of thirty and eight years wait?

Your lips, mine. These arms,
opening. Do you see it now?

Do you? Come to me, then,
and we will trouble the water.

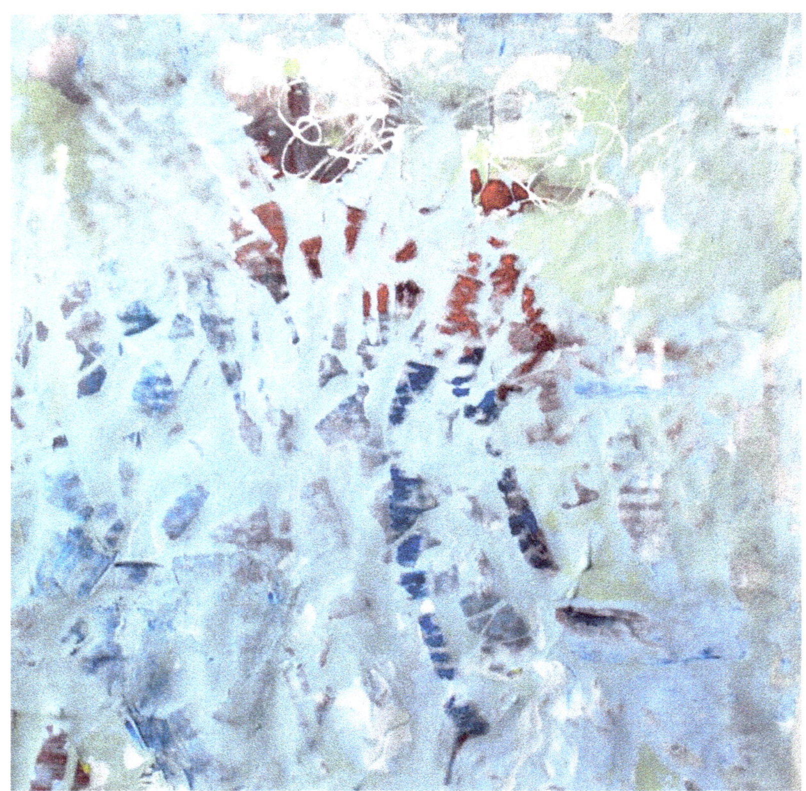

she pondered everything that had happened in her heart

Safe Place to Land

When the angel comes, are we ready? Are our wombs primed
to conceive God, to carry the weight of Him, to thrust Him forth

into this fractured world? Can we wrap our heads around
the conceit of creating the creation of us? Or do we

search for a different mythology, one that lets us off
the hook, one that preaches forget thy neighbor, love only

thyself? Can we reach nirvana
without tramping the mundane? Will we

rock the boat if we stretch out a hand? What if
the fingers that swim towards ours are ours? What if

every face grimacing in pain, every skin and bones child,
every soul crying out for mercy, is us? If we

plug our ears, shut our eyes, will it stop? What if
we are the shepherds and the Christ? The Wise Men

and the star? The Saviour and the saved? What if
heaven and hell be only us? What if we are

all the things that are, now and forevermore?
What if the angel is each and every one of us,

bearing an Annunciation we will ponder
for the rest of our days? What if there is

no safe place to land? No inn, no stable,
no manger? Do we still dare the journey?

Proclaim the good news? Die for
the sake of it, forsaking ourselves?

By God, how can we not.

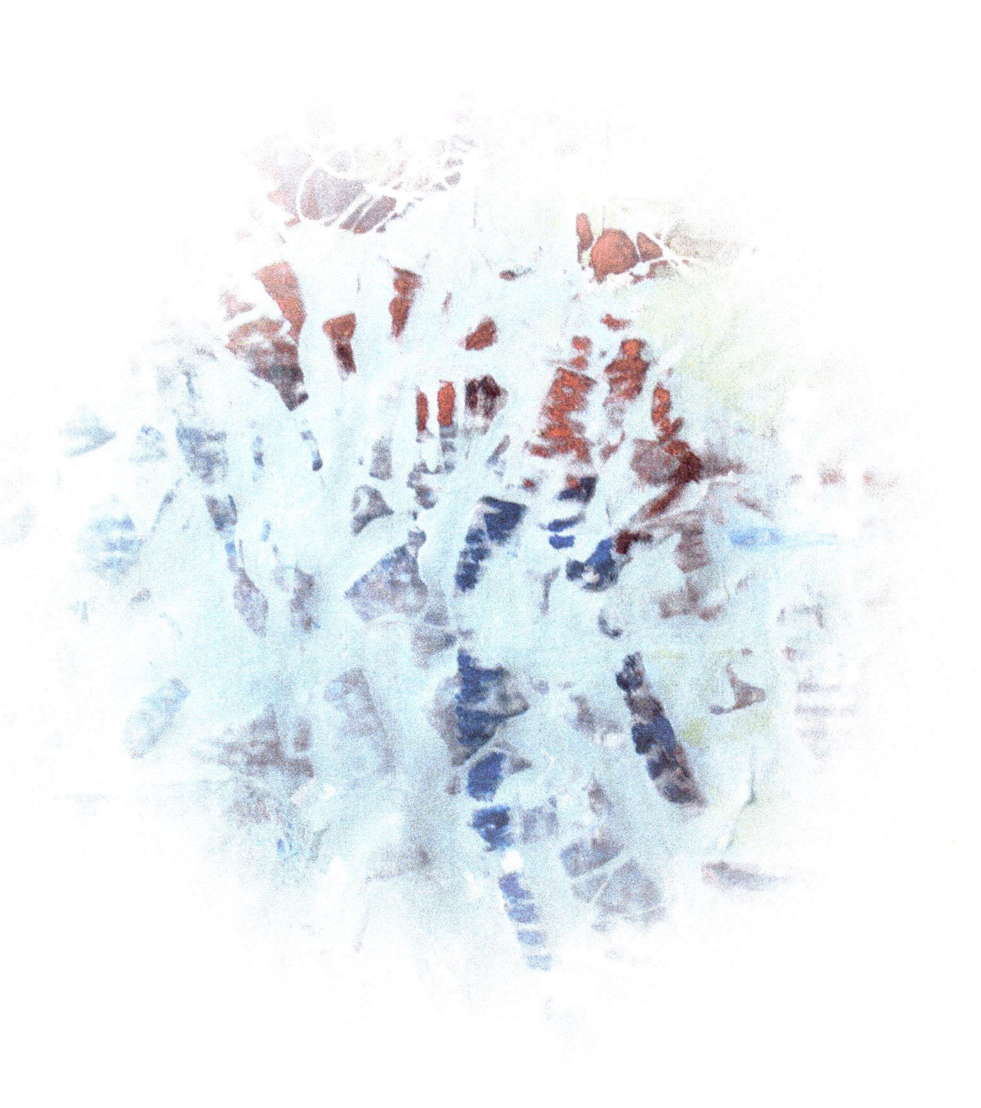

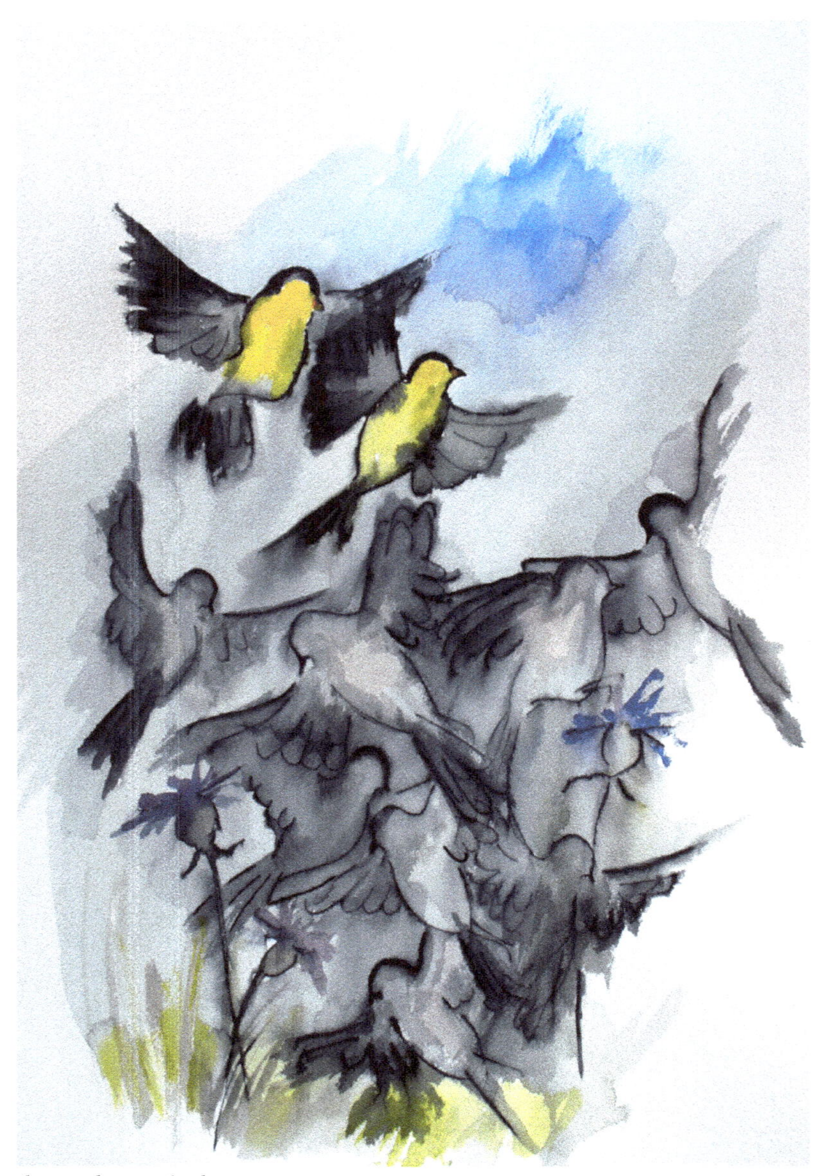

sky people: two finches rise

Escape Velocity

What is needed is to break free,
                pull away,
                rise above.
What is needed is not the drab,
                the ashen,
                the groupthink,
                the gray-headed
                logic of last days.
What is needed comes not singly,
                not on its own
                initiative, not
                unaided, not
                as comes an
                island.
What is needed is the beating wing,
                the fluttering heart,
                the hammering pulse,
                the desire, the pairing,
                two by two,
                the olive leaf transferred
                beak to beak.
What is needed is golden like the meadow
                grass in fall, like
                the plumage of
                two finches, rising,
                like the treasure of
                two hearts, treasured
                by two hearts, liberally spent.
What is needed is a patch of blue, a window
                open in the streaming river
                of heaven through which we
                soar and dive, catch a thistle
                of hope, a seed of the divine.

What is needed is to fold the wings and glide
            between warble and twitter,
            string the perimeter line,
            perch to perch, with song
            and silence.
What is needed is the needful things, the
            empty nests, the lost,
            the misguided, the blind,
            the lame, the hungry, the
            requisite hollow places
            in the body, the buoyancy
            of air in the bones, the
            choiring in the
            vaulted airy places,
            the pulling against
            the gravitas of
            earthly things, the
            I'll be damned-ness
            of us flying
            in the face
            of
What is needed.

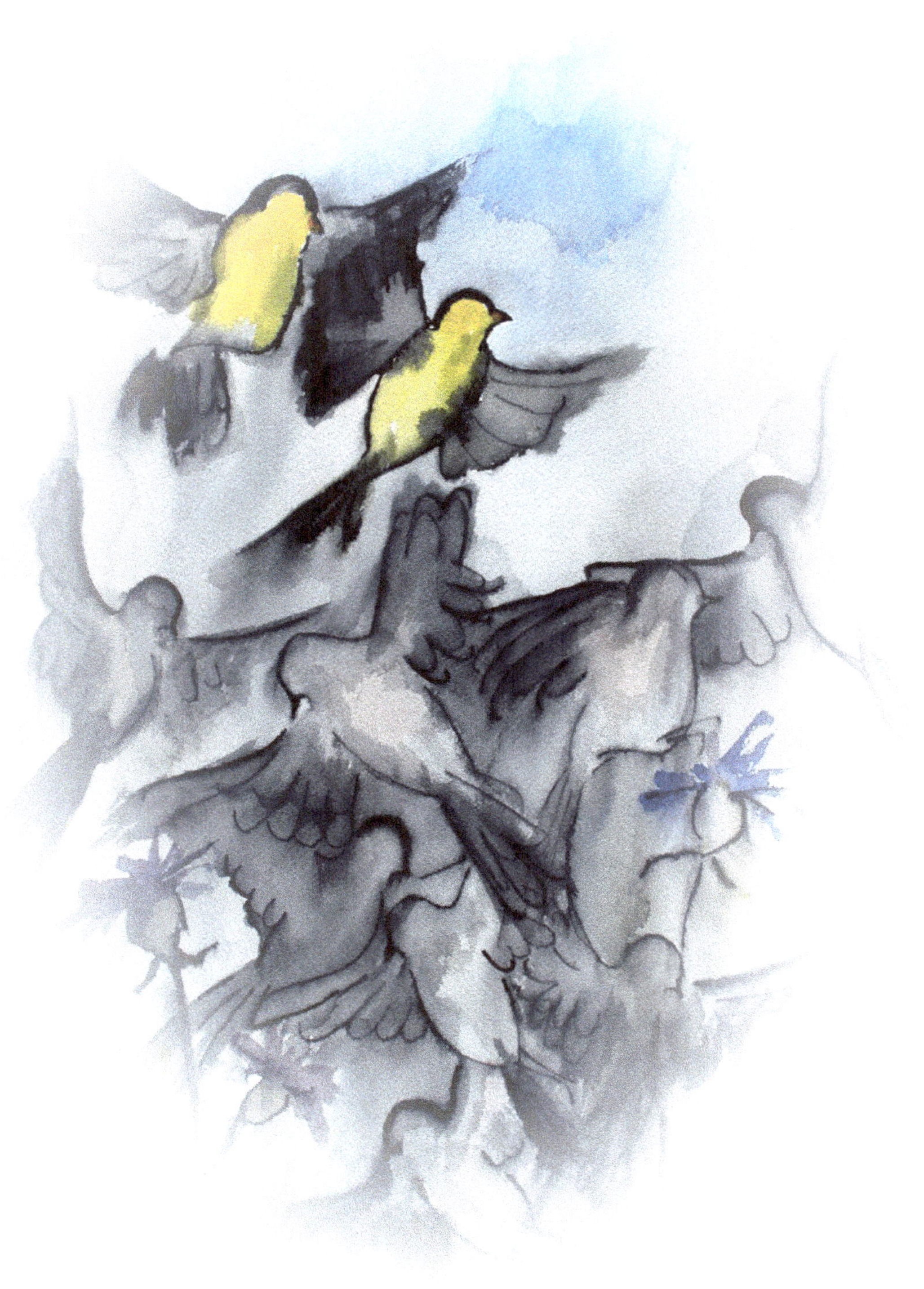

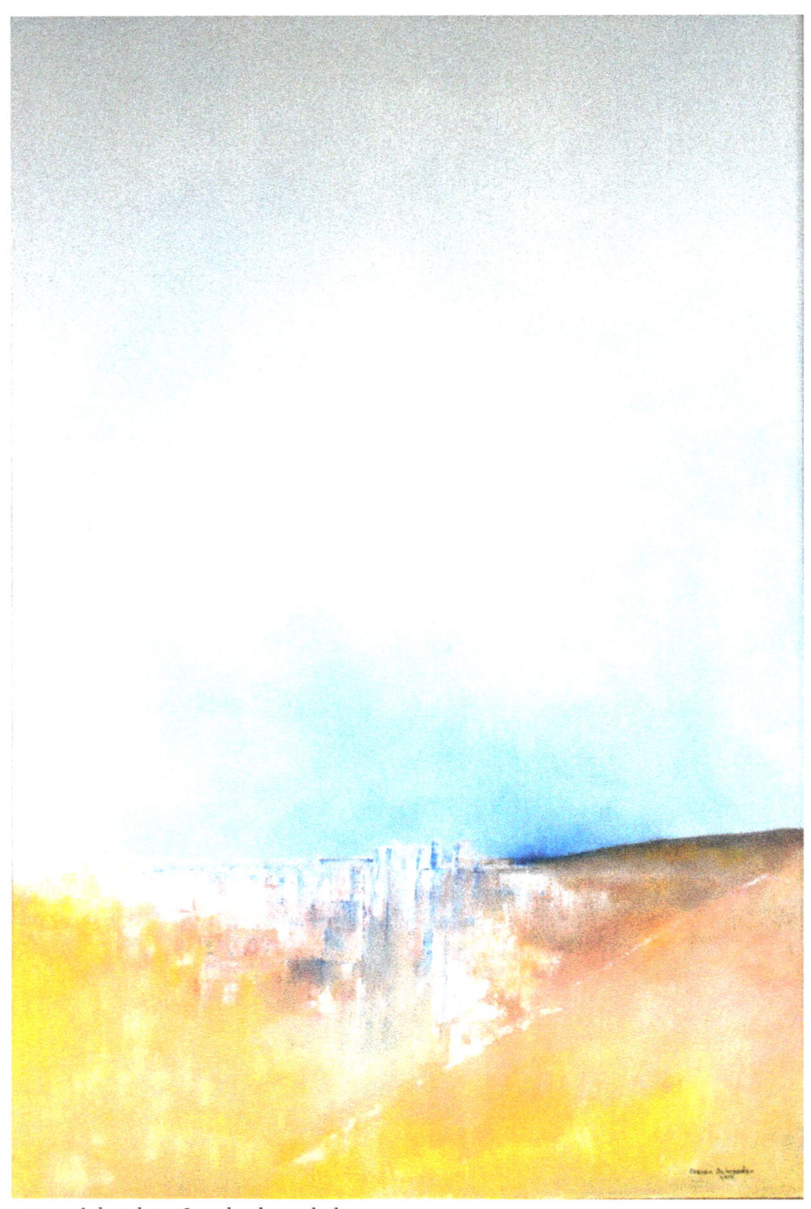

cities of the plain 2: a backward glance

Leaving Dallas (After the Reading)

Spires of glass,
cathedral of the
fast buck, patron

saint of the stop
and go, keeper of
the middle days

of my life, I watch
you fade in the
rear view, knowing that,

finally, a decade after
the first leaving, I've
retrieved some lost piece

of me, something
I forgot to pack before,
a corner of my heart

that said *one day, one
day*—only this is
that day and the

suitcase of me
is full this time,
this exodus leaves

Big D dust
in its wake, the
get-rich-quick

dust, the highway
in the skyway dust.
O tower of Babel,

how could I ever

have loved you?
Cold-armed, barren
wombed, secreter of

ozone, I came,
said my piece,
made my peace

with your dollar-
hungry hands and
ahead somewhere

blue sky opens
big salvation
arms, wind

kisses grass,
cottonwood fluff
drifts free and easy

across the face
of the prairie, the face
of me, dry-eyed, except

for one corner of one
socket, a tiny seedling
of rain, just enough

to nourish this
laying down to rest,
to drown the

muttering of condolences,
dampen the splattering
of earth, ease the knowledge,

the bittersweet certainty,
this time
there is no coming back.

Part Four

Dancing in the Eye

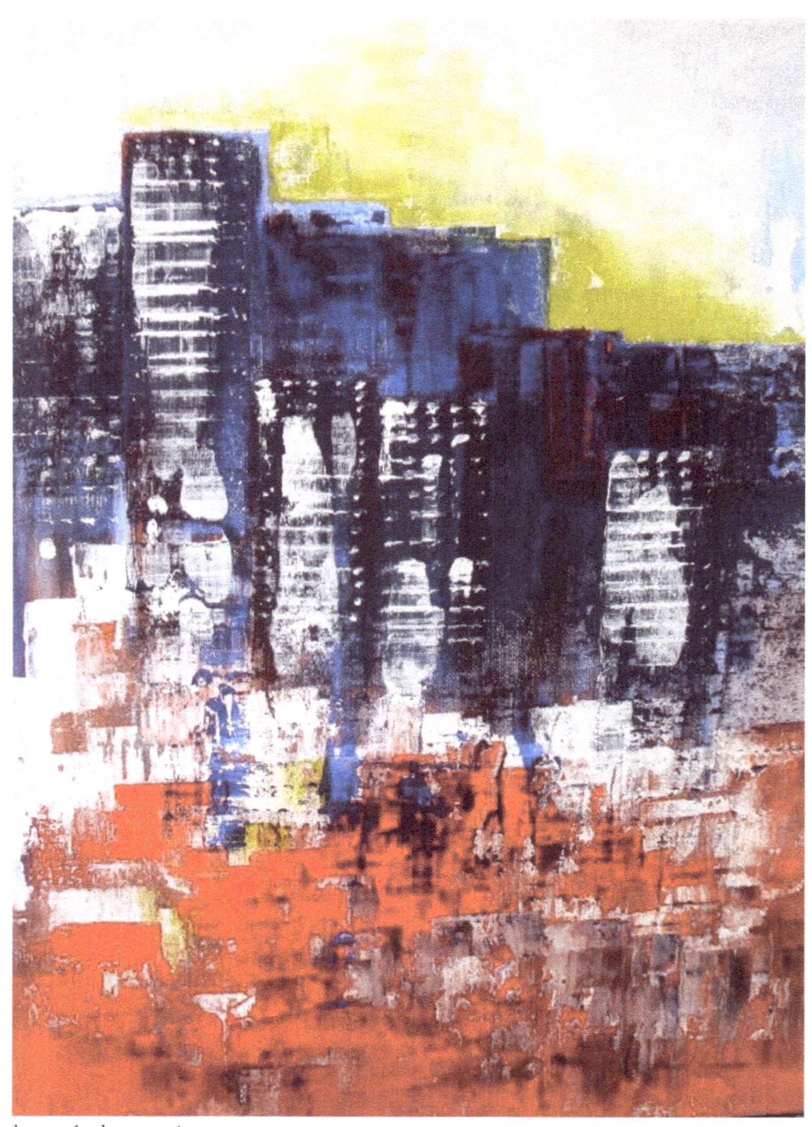

let us find a city 1

Let Us Find a City

But not this one. Too windy,
big-shouldered, reeking
of hog butchery. Too much
blood and guts, sweat and tears,
fear and loathing. We want

an easy city, one whose towers
are not so reflective of the ghostly soul of us.
That's the past, or a present we don't want
to contemplate. Give us the future,
a city of tomorrow. A Walt Disney

city with people movers, because
we are people and we want to be
moved without flexing an emotion.
Give us Alexa, Siri, Uber, Google,
Amazon, DoorDash. Let us grow

fat and lazy and die of diabetes
and heart disease. Let us have
cocktail guests who will worship
at the reliquaries of pristine ellipticals
and always-on 75" LED UHD 4K oracles.

Let us grill on the Fourth and
the Days of Labor and Memory
and blow our ears and eyes and minds
with dahlias and diadems, cakes and
crossettes, and imagine that these

pyrotechnic delicacies
echo cries of legs and arms and torsos
sliced and diced in cities not ours,
cities on the far side of the world
with names that do not roll off

our tastefully erogenous tongues,
as the name of our city shall.
O give us cities named for
ancient railroad men and fathers of
a found country and vanquished

indigenous peoples. O for Pete's sake
give us cities, for we are tired of wandering
the Sinai of empty promises, foodstuffs hailing
from the sky, libations pissing from rocks,
tired of Charlton Heston and his

stony-voiced tablets. Give us a city
of milk and honey, golden
calves, a city on a hill
without the salt of the earth
and the light of the world,

a city with no parables attached,
no Puritanical lectures. Just give us
a city. Any city. We're tired of looking.
Hell, we'll even take Carl's town
if it's still available.

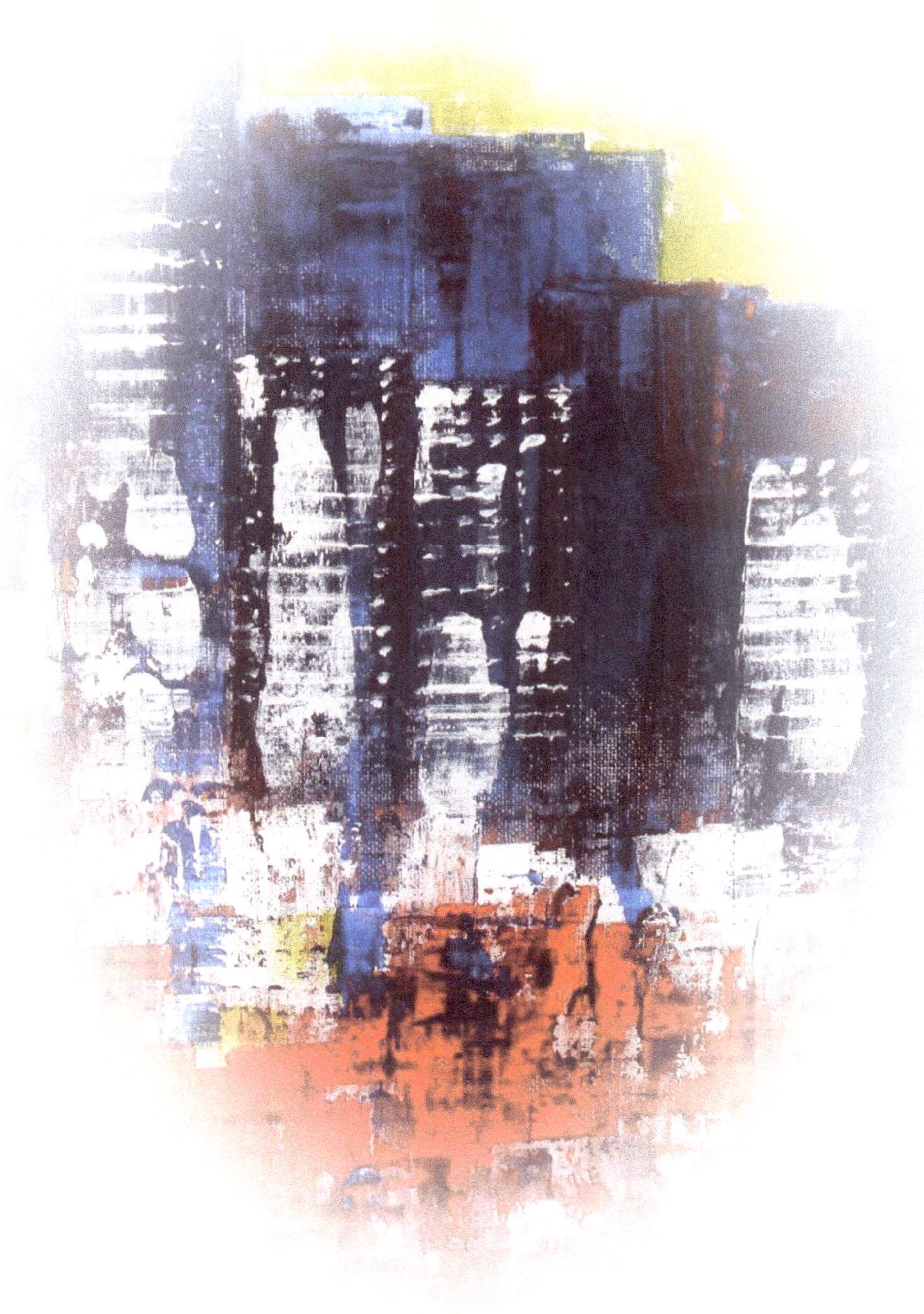

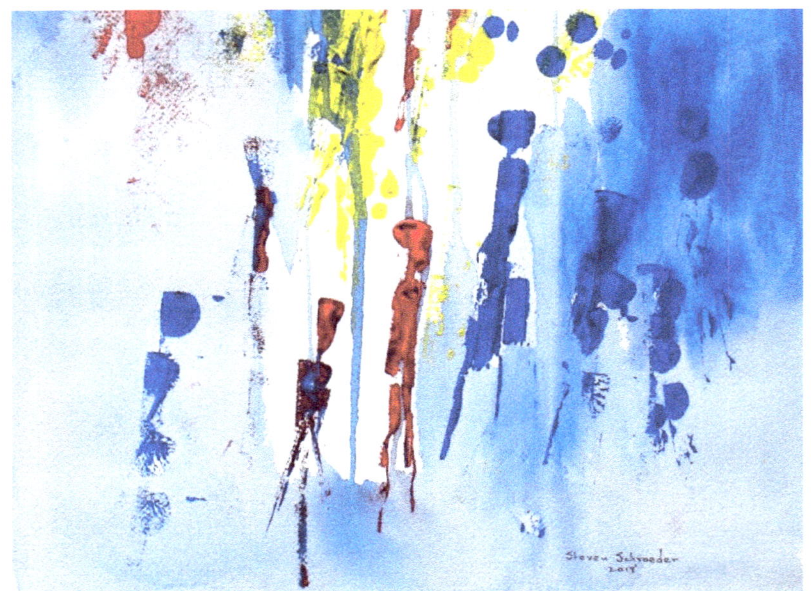

happy workers

Office Party

Some of us are red and some of us
are blue and some of us are other

rainbow colors that didn't make it into
the official version of things
toe the company line

and some of us are fractured,
falling, maybe, from office windows
scraping the sky

though for the most part
we are happy here in the nirvana

of industry, the heaven
of high tech, the holy of holies
of highest finance

                              ladder
                  corporate
            the
climbing

smiling emojis downloaded
from the employee handbook
pasted across our faces

as we take that first step
that last best step

looking over our shoulders at
frowning 401(k)s, pensive pension
buy-outs, tempered glass

ceilings, hoping we got in on the
ground floor, trying not to wonder
what happens when

the elevators are out of order
the stairwells victims

of a hostile takeover, such a
tender offer at first it seems
we bring out the

party whistles, yellow streamers
someone bakes a cake, we all wear

pointy Tin Man hats, Valentine cutouts
tacked to our chests, even the boss

smiles in an A.I. sort of way
hot, cold, lukewarm, we were born
to say

Good morning in passing
on the street, in the hallway, over the walls

of our cubicles, even if it isn't, even if
it isn't us
raking in the big bucks, the dough

the moolah, the Benjamins, even if
we're just worker bees
in the hive

of progress,
humming a happy tune

until the Dow Jones smacks us
with a rolled-up Wall Street Journal,
dispatching us to the achromatic void

at the heart of all things corporate,
that secret graveyard
we whistle our way around Monday through Friday

fingers crossed,
knock on laminate wood.

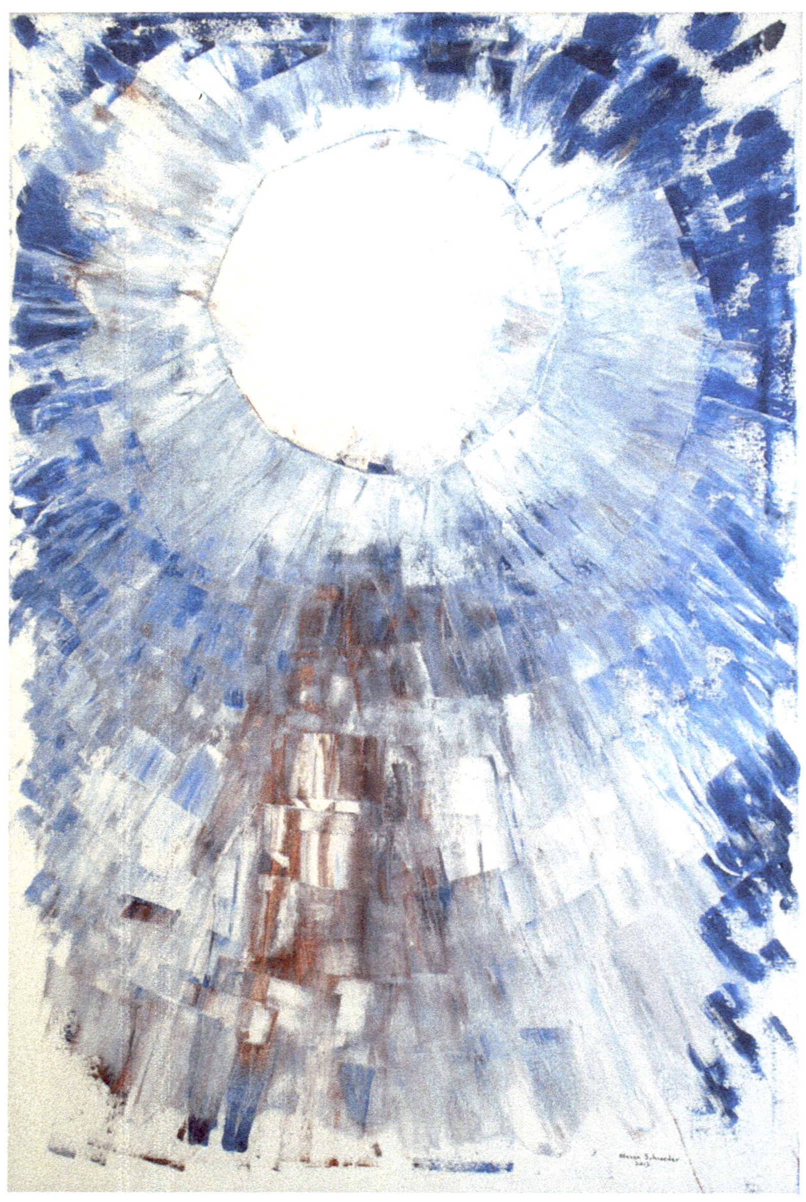

sister moon

Up on the Roof

For Roy and Pat Beckemeyer

Yes, it could be that song
could be

the Drifters, drifting out
of nostalgic transistors
into the blue crystal moonlight of this rooftop,

circa when-we-were-young, you and I spinning,
dancing, twirling hand in hand.

O is that how it happened,
the two of us so innocent then?

Or does memory fail,
moonlight blind,
do dreams fade,

the suns of
strange lands finally arise,
despite our

star struck eyes,
kisses,
caresses,
forever-words exchanged,

exposing the rooftop for what it really is:

empty? All rooftops: empty. All
buildings fallen in. All cities
aged

to wrinkled skin, lost lost-treasure maps, nothing left but

shadows napping in infinite twilight,
loosed balloons of darkness detached. What streets

are these and how did we come
not to know them, what is the meaning
of the absence

of footfalls, the echoes of nothing following, a pall

over these avenues
of old and gray, the cold and frail
boulevards of yesterday?

What stumbling steps
do we dance
into the long night coming, is it

even the same moon,
how can it be,
how can it possibly be
the same tune, it's crazy
what these kids today play—but

it could be. Yes, it could be

that we never left, never came down,
the moon never set, the hand in hand
of us never grew old, never grows
old—could be

that a rooftop is, the moonlight is,
after all, only what we dance on, drift in,

always, if we're lucky.

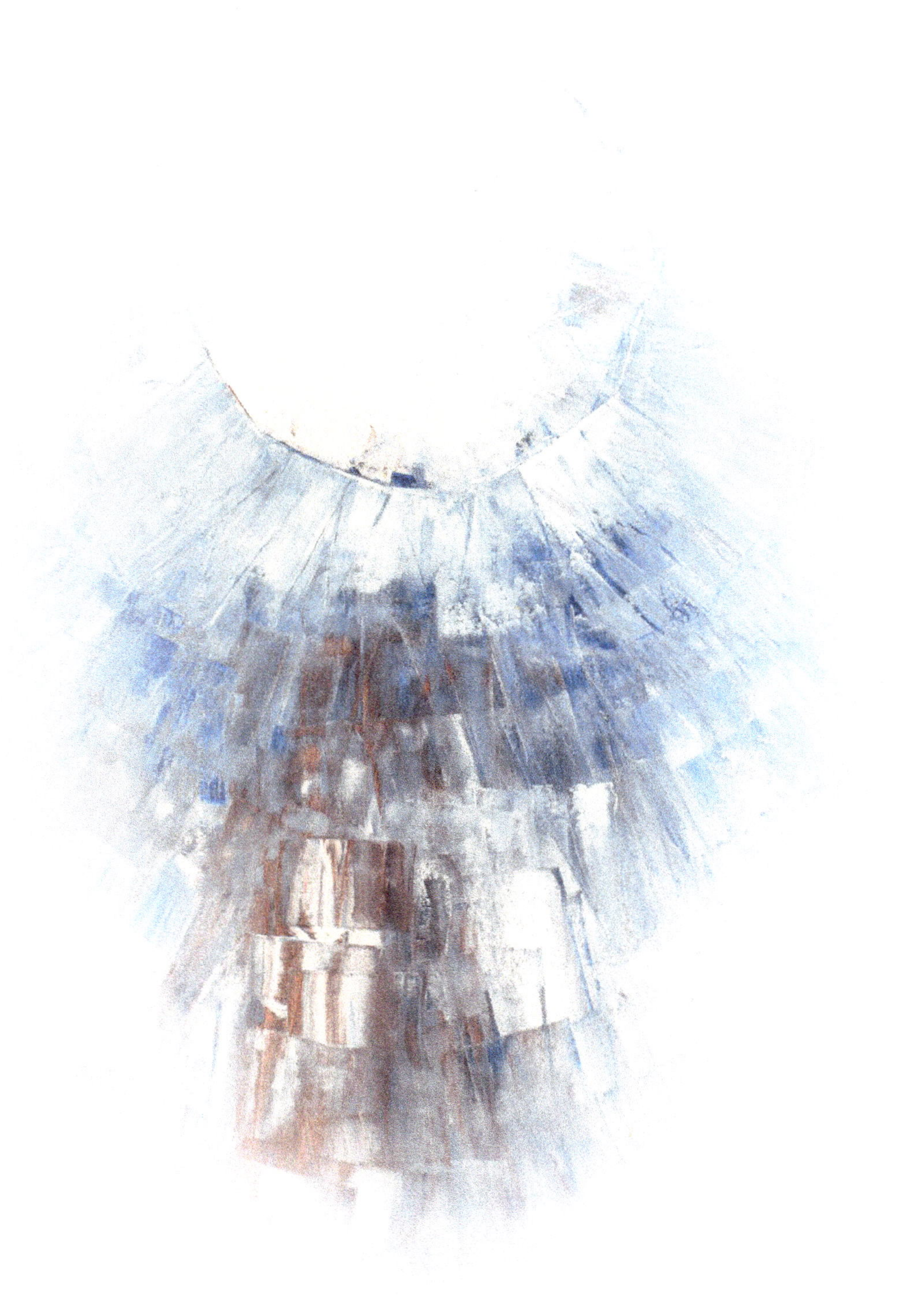

from what i've tasted of desire...

Dancing in the Eye

Fire and ice might suffice
for some, but when I go
I want the world awhirl

with the news of it,
the deafening roar
of my absence-to-be,

good lowland folk
raptured heavenward,
whole cities swept

out to sea, navies
dry-docked on mountain tops,
jumbo jets scrambled like

pick-em-up sticks. I want
cars confettied in whatever trees
it pleases me to leave stand.

I want looting and raping and
pillaging, lines of power
powerless. I want my name

slapped on that twisted sucker
for the record books.
I want you to clap hands

as I spit flamenco defiance
in the eye of my own passing,
Django riffing, guitar on knee,

smoke curling from the
cigarette beneath his
penciled Romani mustache

into the *c'est la vie* of
my next performance.
Tickets going, going,

gone.

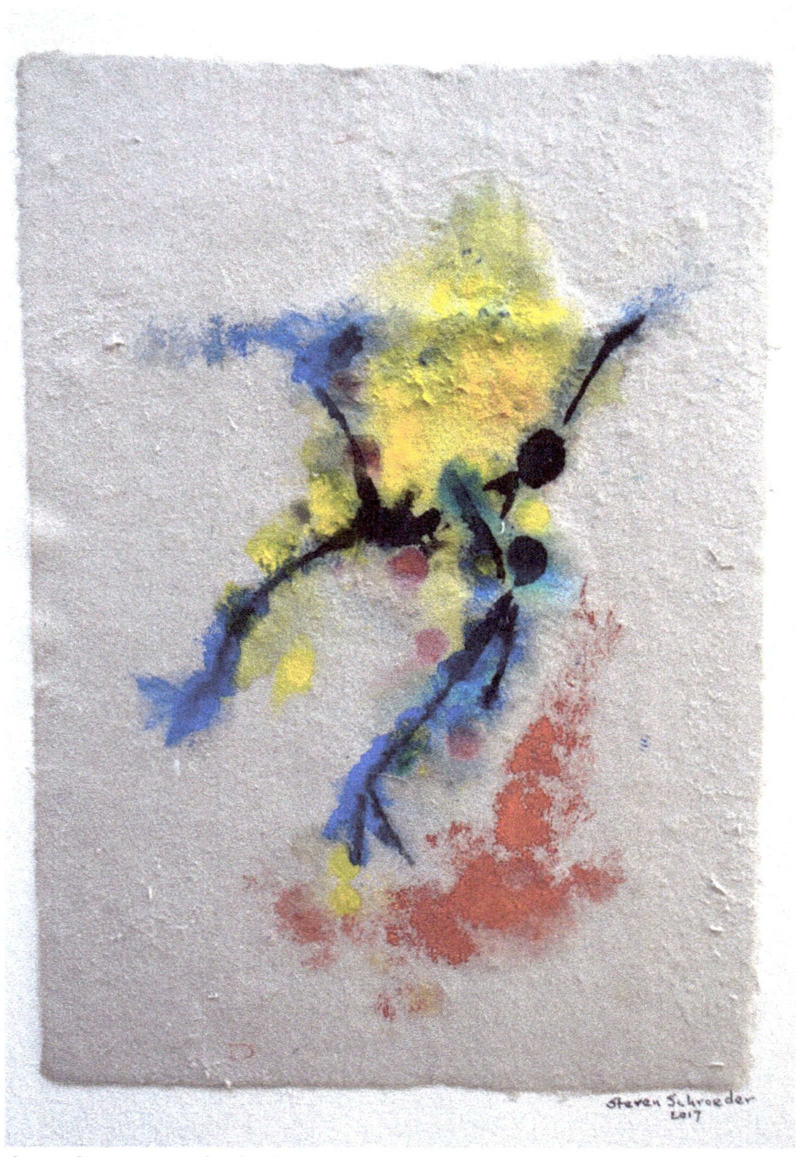

the arc between two deaths 5

Fall from Grace

The aerialist will not be performing tomorrow.

The aerialist will not be performing next week.

The aerialist will not be performing a second act.

The aerialist has fallen. Gracefully, but fallen. Splattered,
gracefully. Gracefully smeared blood across the carnival floor.

The aerialist has fallen. Whether from tightrope, trapeze,
matters not. What matters is the plunge, the graceful arc
of it, the head-first-ness, the absence of scream on the way
down, the acceptance that, yes, the alternate reality
is no longer alternate.

The aerialist has fallen, again. The aerialist never uses
a net. The aerialist dies a little each time. This is the reality
of alternates. What we can learn from the aerialist.

The aerialist has fallen, despite studying with the Flying Wallendas,
Doris Humphrey, the Dalai Lama. The aerialist will fall
again, in the next reality, no alternative. Need we not cry out
in horror. The aerialist lives to fall. Strings, death to death,
the wire of grace. Reaches for the bar of heaven, existence
to existence.

The aerialist reads Nietzsche on the way down, gracefully turning
the pages of *Also sprach Zarathustra*, which has been extracted from
blue leotard waistband at the first slip of foot, hand. The aerialist only captures
a few words, maybe a sentence, before time runs out. The next fall,
a few more. The aerialist is anxious to see how it ends, this paean to
eternal return, how it can be merely physical, sans Samsara. The aerialist
is skeptical. The aerialist has much experience with falling. There is a beauty
to it. A skill. In the last instant, a suspension of time and space, a feeling of
falling *into* grace. As if being born especially for this moment. This arc.
This death.

The aerialist will be performing, in the next reality, under a big top
near you.

Part Five

Chasing the Sun

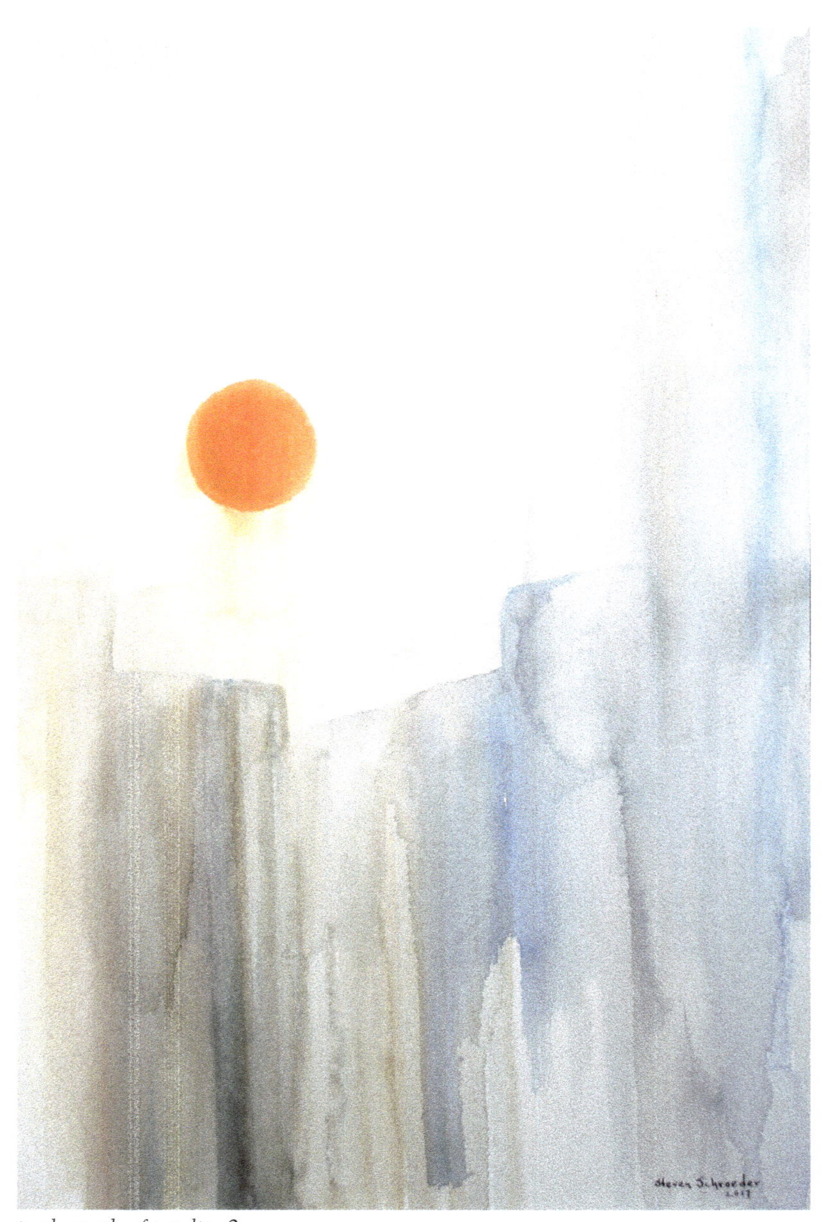

in the path of totality 2

All That is Solid

On this day we exist
and on this day only.
The ghosts we have built loom
into half remembered
skies, crowd us, hem us in,
but they speak not
for today, and tomorrow
is deaf, and yesterday dead.
We float. We drift. We shine,
sometimes. Illumine worlds, sometimes.
On this day, this one day of us,
what bright-tongued words
do we have to offer?
Can we speak fast enough
to beat the nightfall, elucidate
ourselves before we
wink out, blaze our names
across misted skies,
mystery cities—did we
once live here? What do we know
of being? Do we reach out and touch
being? Does being reach out and touch
us? Do we live in being or being
in us? Are we, in fact, being?
The ghosts whisper: *We are*
you. We are the night
in the day. We are the before
and the after. We are.
You cannot be without us.
O we would like to negate them,
we would. But we have only
this day, and this day only.

Refutation of ghosts
is a tedious thing,
and we float, we drift,
we shine, we let
no anchors drag us
down. Now belongs
to us, and it is all
we have. We flare
and flux. Flux and
flare. All that is solid
melts as we pass.
We are light, we are
air, we will live forever.
We are us in our own
image, and on this day,
this one day, we can be
everything.

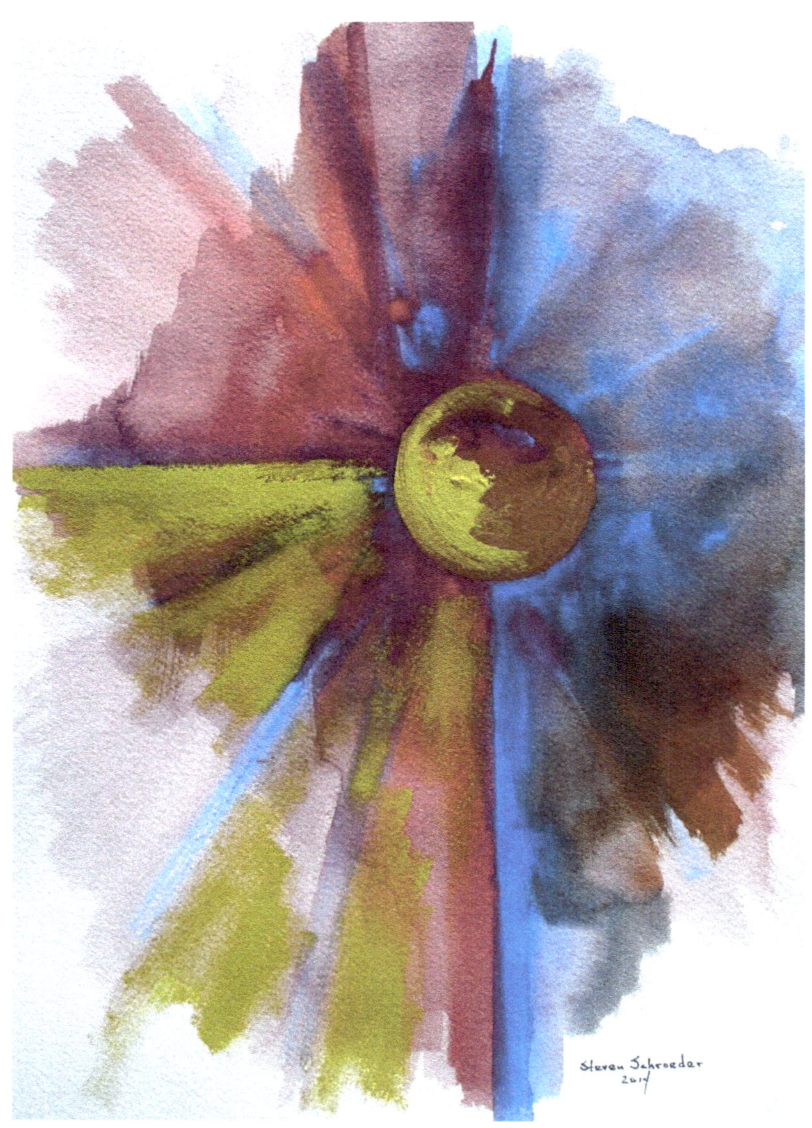

solstice

Love Letter

Dearest —,

I think that for this communique a text over the TDRS will
not do.

      Here at the bottom of the world it is night 24/7 but
the stars, oh my, the stars! I look at them and think of you,
sitting in your prefab igloo on top of the world, doomed to see
only the one star, the same inquisitorial light all day and night.
How boring, how utterly dreamless it must be. Here we have a
brilliant jade ribbon, the Aurora Australis, literally dancing
across the sky and I think of your eyes, and how shy you were
when we went to that club in Westport for the first time and
you refused to get out on the floor with me. Boy did I make a
fool of myself! But at least I got you to laugh. How I miss that
laugh. When I go out and see the red lights we use to keep
from interfering with the CMB studies playing on the walls of
the station, I can't help but remember how your hair smells
and how much longer it is—how much longer it threatens to
be—before I can bury my face in it again. I know you will blush
at that last—you need to get your mind out of the gutter! Did I
ever mention that your laugh sounds like an Emperor
penguin's mating call? Not that you would know, as you don't
have any of the tuxedoed clowns up there. We have a colony
not too far from us over at Taylor Glacier. You should see how
deeply they bow to each other before copulation, like at the
tea ceremony when we were in Kyoto—no, scratch that. I don't
want to put ideas into your head. I will not spend the winter
incubating our next egg while you're off cavorting the seven
seas. Scratch that, too. I shouldn't have brought it up.

But I must bring it up. I must tell you, if only to get it off my chest, last time I was at the colony, a sad thing happened, a thing that can only be told with pen and paper, even though you will not like to read it, and the next Hercules will not come till October. A female was transferring the egg to its mate when the egg fell and, well, thick as the shells are, the egg cracked, and, with the temps being what they are here—well, let's just say it was gut-wrenching to watch the two of them waddle back to the sea on separate paths, knowing their time together was over. I couldn't help but think of Jason, how tiny he was, how little time we had with him, how you never got the chance to hold him. How you staid with your sister for those long weeks after. How lonely the house was. How total the darkness. I swear, even the bed wept beneath me. How much I felt at fault, somehow. How bright the day when you finally returned home! How it darkened again when you suggested separate postings.

Akihiko sticks his head in to say the SPT has picked up something interesting. I must close so I can take a look. Perhaps a new galaxy cluster? If so, I think you know what I will name it, if I have any say in the matter, and by God I better.

Tell Santa when you see him I've been a good boy.

Love always, —

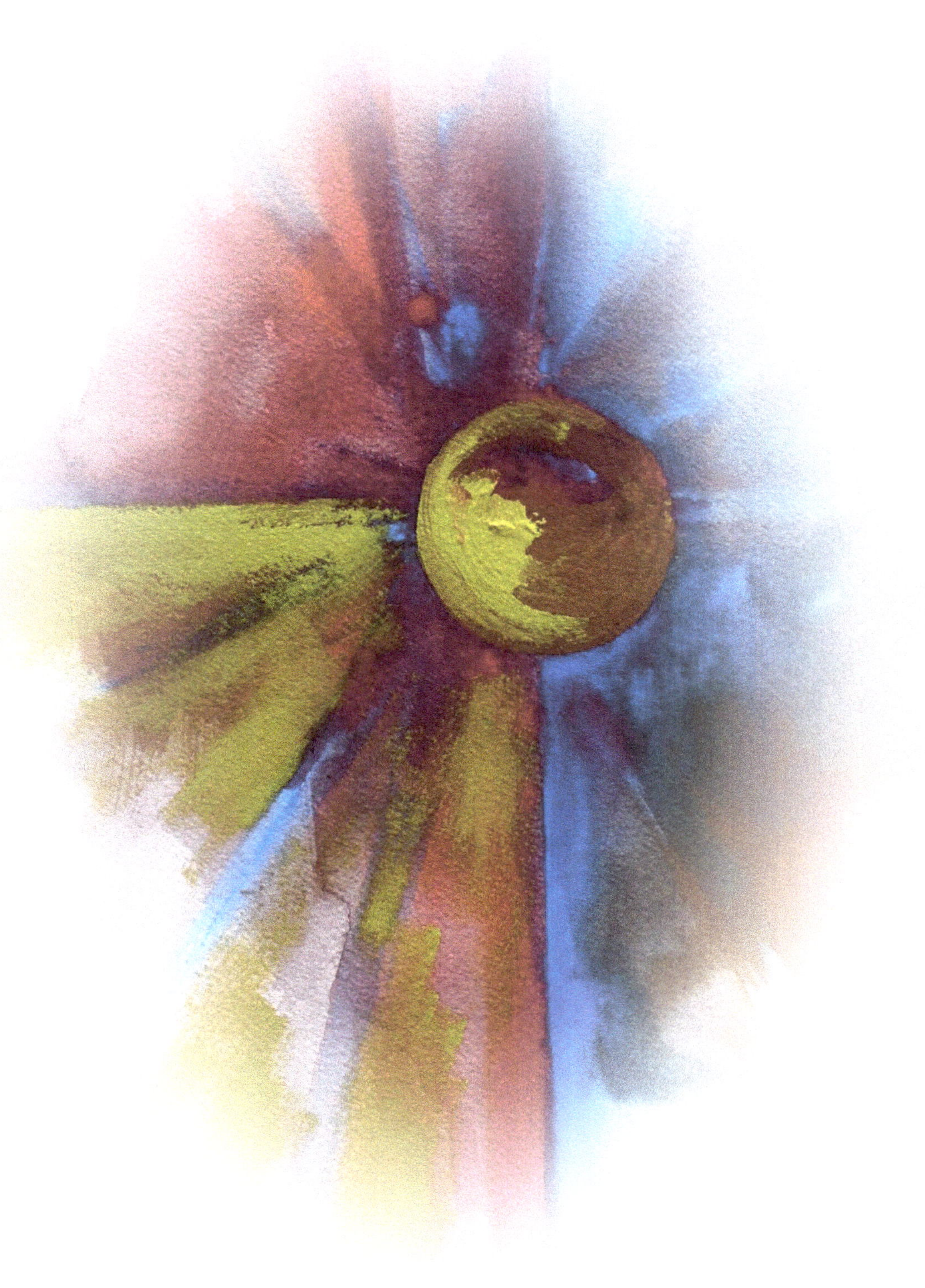

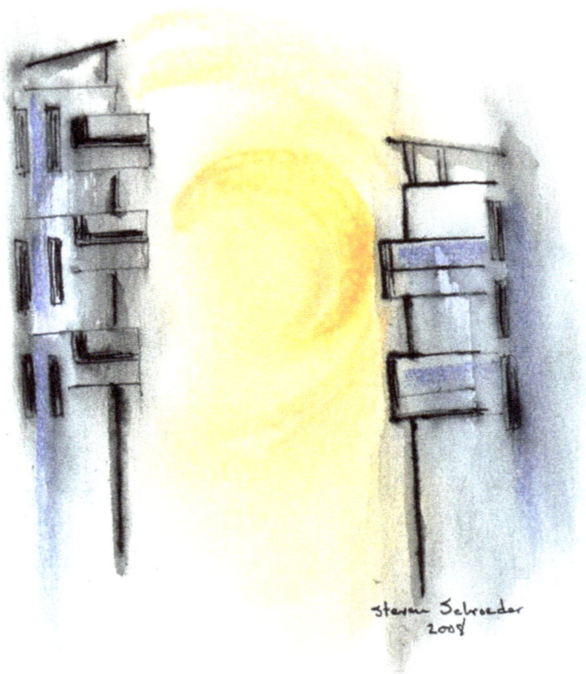

east, rising 4

Morning After

All mornings are after
but this morning especially, with this
view as we stand on the balcony
coffee cups in hand, looking up

the boulevard towards a birth
we have never fully appreciated
the way we do this morning
not having done what we did

last night, not before, not together
though we knew it would come about
had we stopped to think about it
we thought about nothing last night

certainly not this sunrise, the next
sunrise and all the rising suns to follow
how changed the world would look
this first morning after, or is it we

who are changed, accidental midwives
blindly laboring for fly-by-night ecstasy
during what is now the flown night before
or perhaps it is we who are after

as in *happily ever*, as in
what we were previously
separate, other, two suns
in a sky built for one

after coffee what we will do
up for grabs until my fingers
feel yours searching, interlocking
and we retreat, our children

the boulevard, penthouses, sun
the future, can fend for themselves
this first morning, after, after all
knows no time of day.

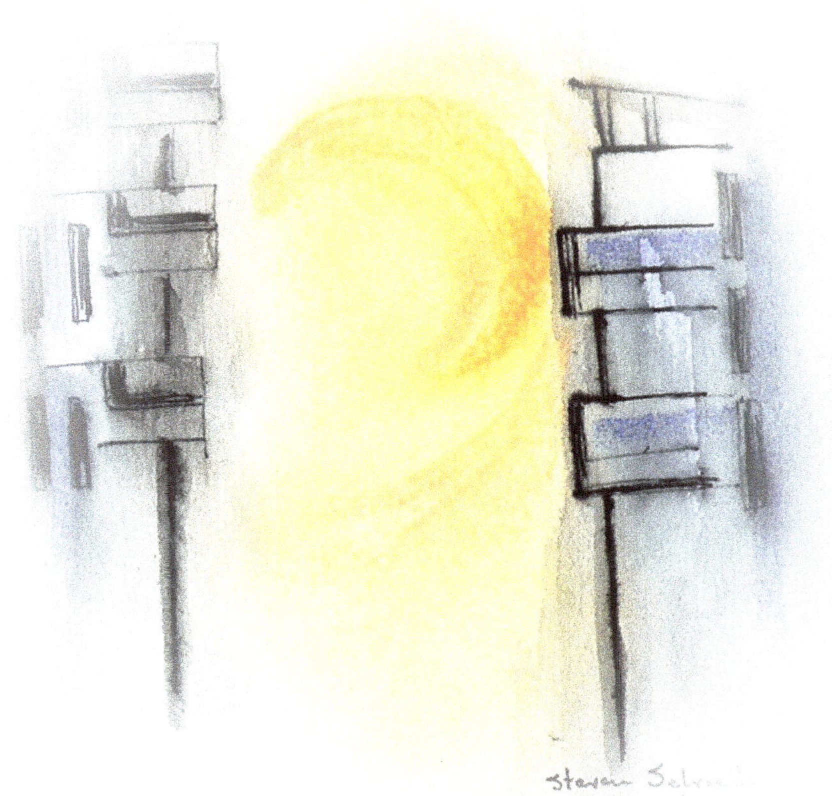

empty promises 1

Cloudy with a Chance of Miracles

When we see this, when we
pass through this landscape

on the way from wherever
we've been to wherever

we'd rather be, and pronounce it
dismal, forsaken, unloved,

are we really seeing
what the artist has portrayed,

or projecting some Waiting-For-
Godot play of ourselves

onto the proscenium stage
of heaven? Do we recognize

the portent of the end of drouth,
the harbinger

of a bumper crop, the birthing
of the breadbasket of a world,

the care and feeding
of a multitude, the famine

in our souls, the thirst
for a taste of the bloody-browed tears

of God? Or do we, like Peter, let the storm
of doubt sink us, conjure up

a cyclone of self-pity, a whirlwind
of whys and wherefores, a twister

of what ifs, the slow drain
on the promise of youth, the seeming wasteland

of a delusion that, even now, we are
headed somewhere, have been

somewhere? If only we could recognize this place
for what it is: not a forecast

of clock-ticks past or present,
but the here and there of us,

the hither and yon moment
we are meant to dwell in always, with all its

murkiness, shadow, veiled suns,
its half-full-or-half-emptiness irrelevant

to the fact of us, at last, stepping through
the spun sugar cobwebs

of that self-constructed
phantom fourth wall,

lowering the window,
and breathing deeply in

the wonder of an expectant sky.

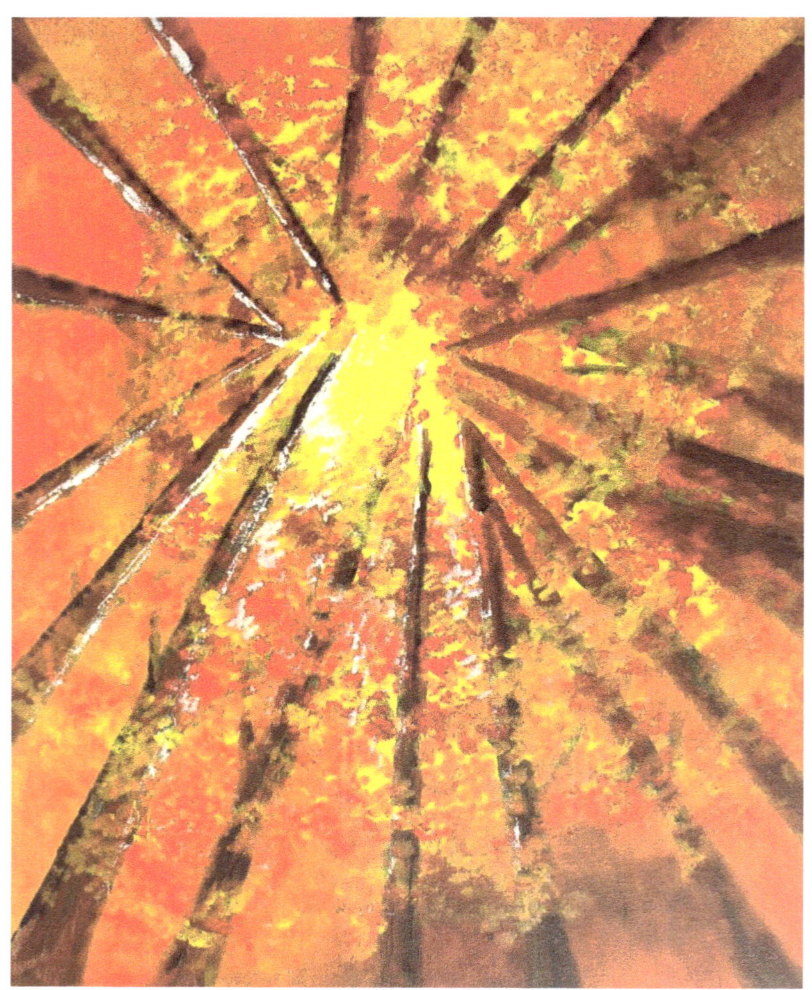

a living mirror

Rain

God is crying. I cup
my hands. Immortal tears pool

in the crucible
of mortality. An image coalesces,

shimmering, an uneasy
reflection as if in a warped

looking glass. But it
cannot be my creation, these tall

timbers soaring up
into the fire and blood of sky

unseen on this
day of death and shadows, this

funereal farewell
to all I've loved and lost, to you,

to me, to us. O
what is it I see here, hold,

slipping slowly
through my fingers, in the palms

of my hands?
Do I sing with Leibniz

the best of all
possible worlds? Would God weep

over such wonderful
spontaneity as the death of love?

I raise the bowl
of flesh to my lips, drink, taste

the admixture
of salt with the holy, know these tears

as mine, sunder
my hands, walk away from heaven.

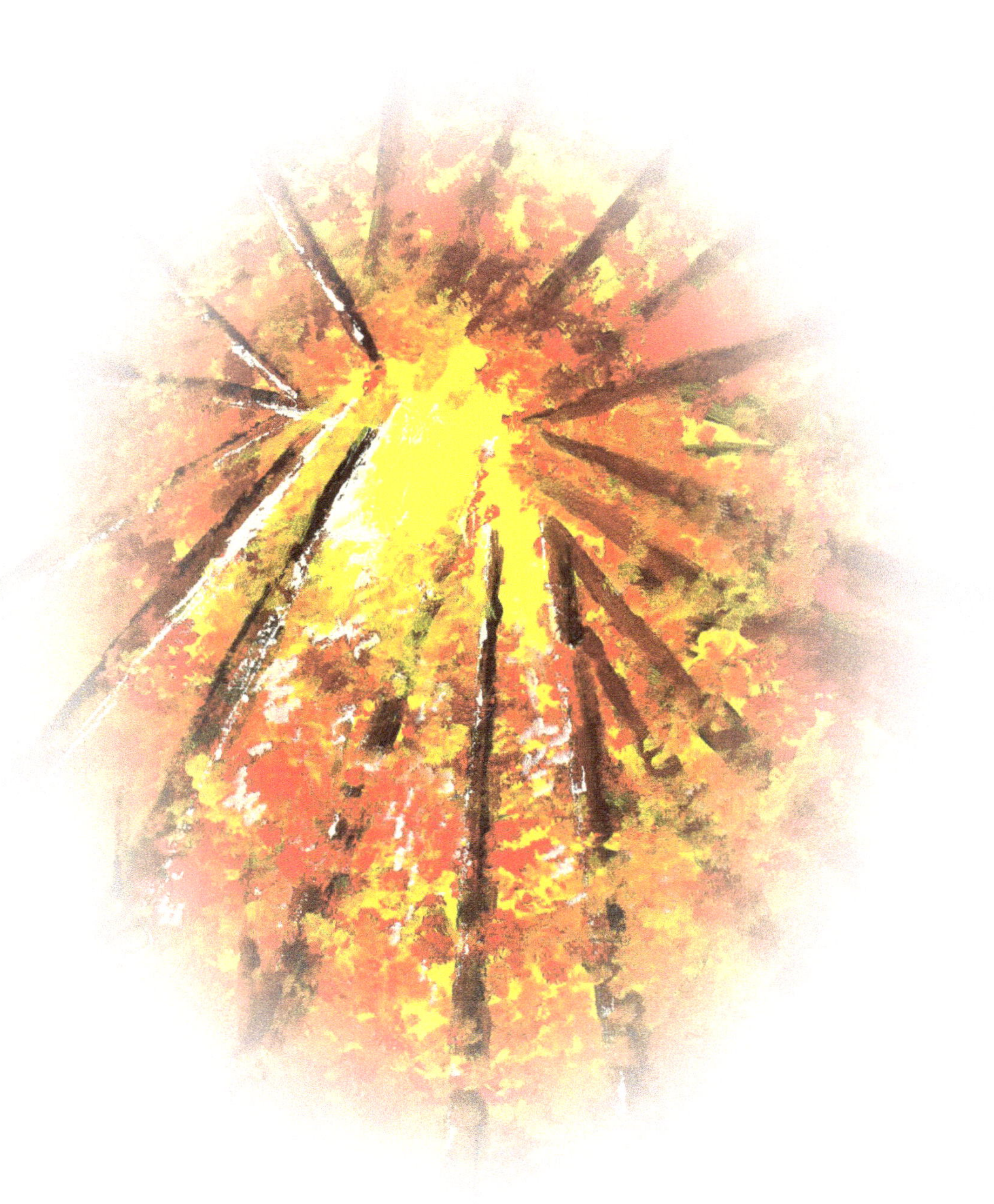

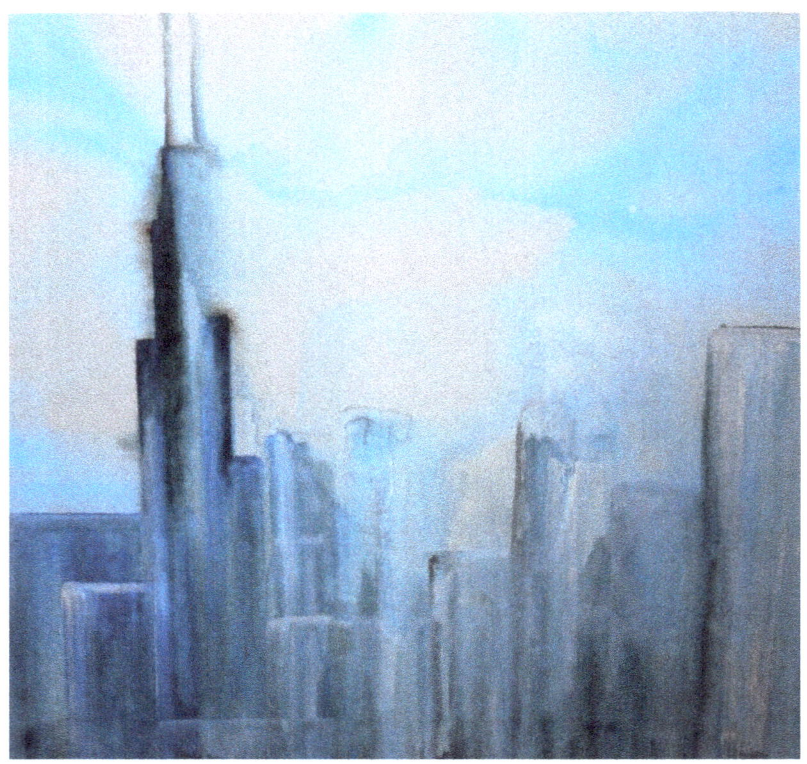

gray city

Chasing the Sun

Somewhere out of sight
at the bottoms of these canyons
are the streets

the pathways of us, furled
parasols in hopeful hands
blazing trails to

something we can't quite
make out
the future, maybe

or some other
one of us
seeking shelter

in this phantom city
of tomorrow bequeathed to us
by the fathers of yesteryear

our spires, our stamens
thirsting for light
cross-pollination

with the stigma of gods
those clouds, could they be
embryos of what's to come

the fruit of us
as we slip into
some corner café

sip from reflecting pools
of coffee cups, map out
sun-soaked concourses

down which demigods of
after-us stroll, heedless, in
our abstraction, of our own

faces of awe and wonder
shining up from
the sultry black depths

clack
metal against ceramic
and we are gone

last day of winter

The End

If you get here before I do,
arrive at this last brutal, brittle day
and you cannot see your way

through the drifts and fogs
of winter, if you are sure
this is it, there is nothing

on the other side of the
icy pond at the end
of the trail and no skates

to reach it with, that everything
you have done has been
in vain, that no one will

remember you once you fade
into the scratchy blur of this
last blue-gray day, that you have

lived a life
of no more consequence
than a flake melting on contact

with your tongue, just remember
how glorious it was when we were young
and flexed those muscular appendages,

what the fleeting falling stars tasted like,
how each moment in each season of your life
enriched the banquet that is you,

the full course that you have become,
and I assure you those who partook of you
are sated for now and evermore, as will be I

when you take my shivering hand
and point me towards that faintest blush
of spring, coming for us only just now

like a new birthed day, all roseate and fresh,
the infant of us, united, finally—come,
let's make snow angels before we go.

Notes

Page 34: *Still Life with Roman Noir.* The painting's title is after a poem by Liang Huichun.

Page 57: *In the Time of Falling Fire.* The poem's title is taken from the last line of Paul Bowers' poem *Fleeing the Oklahoma Panhandle in Summer.* The Greek quotation in the body of Steven Schroeder's painting is from Euripides' *The Trojan Women,* spoken by Hecuba—"There is nothing burning but my crazy child Cassandra racing towards us."

Page 73: *What is the Frequency, Kenneth?* On October 4, 1986, CBS news anchorman Dan Rather was attacked by two men, one of whom repeatedly shouted "Kenneth, what's the frequency?" Eight years later a North Carolina man shot and killed an NBC stagehand. When the shooter was arrested, he admitted to the earlier attack on Rather. He claimed to be a time-traveler from the year 2265 with a chip implanted in his brain and that NBC had been beaming hostile transmissions into his head for years, and that Rather resembled the Vice-President from his own timeline, Kenneth Burrows. Nothing is known about the supposed second man.

Page 86: *Windmill.* The painting's title is from *The Daodejing: A New Interpretation by David Breeden, Steven Schroeder, and Wally Swist,* Lamar University Press, 2015.

Page 94: *What I Remember.* The painting's title is from Karl Marx and Friedrich Engels.

Page 104: *Safe Place to Land.* The painting's title is the artist's translation of a Greek phrase included in Luke/Acts.

Page 118: *Let Us Find a City*. The painting's title is from Carl Sandburg, *The Windy City*.

Page 126: *Up on the Roof*. The painting's title is from Francis of Assisi, *Canticle of the Creatures*.

Page 130: *Dancing in the Eye*. The painting's title is from Robert Frost, *Fire and Ice*.

Page 135: *Fall from Grace*. Doris Humphrey was an early 20th century American dancer and choreographer who developed the theory of "Fall and Recovery," also known as "The arc between two deaths."

Page 143: *Love Letter*. TDRS stands for Tracking and Data Relay Satellite. CMB stands for Cosmic Microwave Background. SPT stands for South Pole Telescope.

Page 154: *Rain*. The painting's title is from Leibniz, *Principes de la nature et de la grâce fondés en raison*, where he writes that "every monad is a living mirror."

About the Author

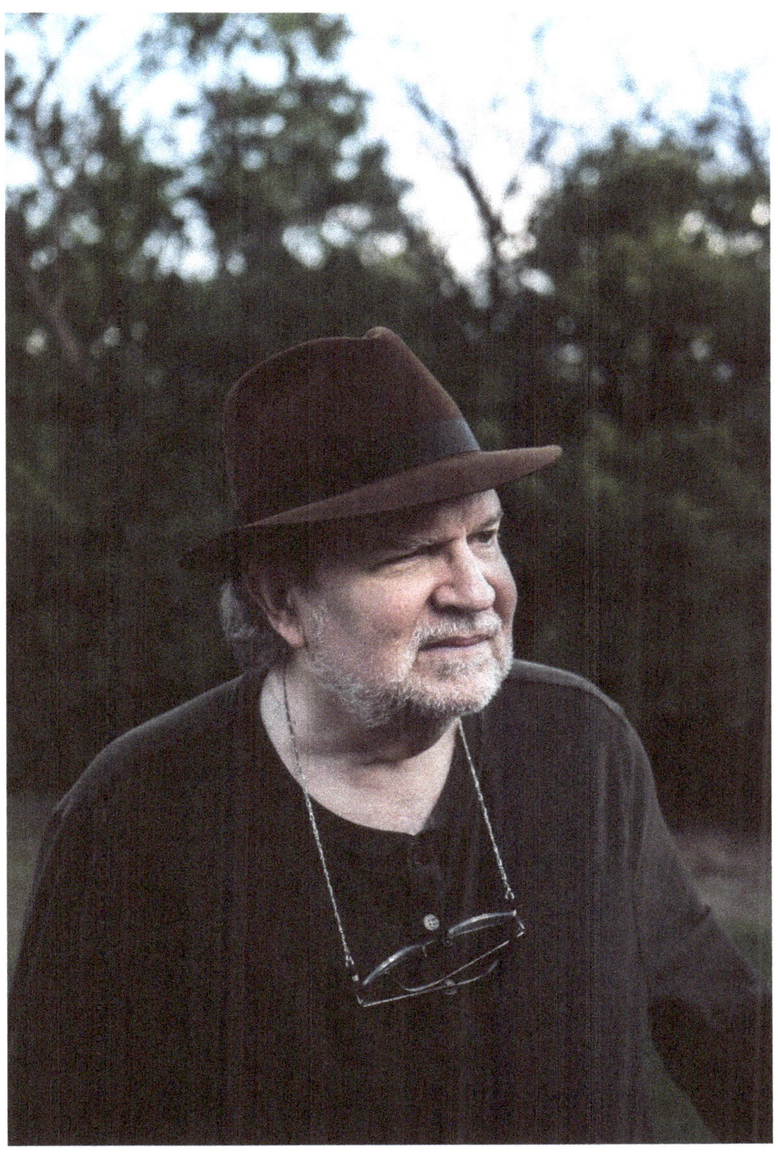

Robert L. Dean, Jr. is the author of *At the Lake with Heisenberg* (Spartan Press, 2018). His work has appeared or is forthcoming in *Flint Hills Review*, *I-70 Review*, *Chiron Review*, *The Ekphrastic Review*, *Shot Glass*, *Illya's Honey*, *Red River Review*, *KYSO Flash*, *MacQueen's Quinterly*, *River City Poetry*, *Heartland! Poetry of Love, Resistance & Solidarity*, and the *Wichita Broadside Project*. He is a multiple *Best of the Net* nominee and a *Pushcart* nominee for 2019. He was a quarter-finalist in the 2018 Nimrod Pablo Neruda Prize for Poetry. He read at the Scissortail Creative Writing Festival and the Chikaskia Literary Festival in 2018 and 2019. He is event coordinator for *Epistrophy: An Afternoon of Poetry and Improvised Music*, held annually in Wichita, Kansas. A native Kansan, he has been a professional musician and worked at The Dallas Morning News. He lives in a one-hundred-year-old stone building in Augusta, Kansas, along with a universe of several hundred books, CDs, LPs, two electric basses and a couple dozen hats. In his spare time, he practices the time-honored art of hermitry.

A Personal Note from the Author

I first met the artist, Steven Schroeder, at the Scissortail Creative Writing Festival, held on the Eastern Oklahoma University campus in Ada, Oklahoma, in April 2018. Steve had an art exhibit at the Grandview Event Center in Ada, and I fell in love with "Leap of Faith" at first sight and asked if I could write a poem to the painting. Steve said yes, and, after some wheeling and dealing, I ended up with the painting hanging on my living room wall, and permission to write to more of Steve's art. "Ghost Town" and "Windmill" followed in quick succession, and, over the succeeding year and a half, the rest of the works contained in this volume came to life. It should be noted that all of Steve's art was composed prior to and independently of the texts in this book. In that sense, this book is not a "true collaboration" but a case of a verbal artist inspired by a sense of kinship with a visual artist's way of seeing. Paul Bowers, another Scissortail and Chikaskia regular, and mutual friend, graciously agreed to publish the resulting manuscript, along with the art, through his indie press. In addition to Paul and Steve, the author wishes to thank Roy & Pat Beckemeyer, Diane Wahto, Skyler Lovelace, Dave Cook, Melany Pearce, Carol Whitaker, Denise Bowers, and Clare MacQueen for valuable insight during the composition of some of these works, as well as Ken Hada at the Scissortail Creative Writing Festival, and Don Stinson and Paul Bowers at the Chikaskia Literary Festival, where some of these works were first presented in front of an audience.

Robert L. Dean, Jr.

Artist's Statement

I am a poet and visual artist who spent many years moonlighting as a philosophy professor. I think of my work as an intersection of chance with design — a collaboration with the media, painting with light while celebrating the way(s) pigment takes to surface, not showing or telling so much as opening a space for a play of possibility.

I am interested in the way light breaks on edges, the way pigment takes to surface, the way words tumble out onto the page, the way the eye of the ear sees them.

I find common ground with John Cage when he says "I have nothing to say and I am saying it and that is poetry" and (in the same piece, his "Lecture on Nothing") when he says "Kansas is like nothing on earth." Kansas, southeastern Colorado, the northeastern corner of New Mexico, the panhandle of Oklahoma, and (especially) the panhandle of Texas – that is where I grew up, and it shaped my eyes like nothing on earth.

I find common ground with Helen Frankenthaler when she embraces chance and lets paint flow on raw canvas to create forms that surprise and invite us to see worlds we would never have seen alone. This leads me to embrace lyric poetry as a form of abstraction (in the way that computer scientists use the term), a simplification (and an interface) that allows us to manipulate complexities below the surface without getting bogged down in them. And it leads me to agree with Georgia O'Keeffe when she says all painting is abstract.

I often find myself spending as much time on what is not there as on what is. This usually means focusing on a single image and letting the whole composition spring up around it — not a narrative but an all at once that evokes a here and now that is, here, now, neither. A likely story is likely to grow out of this when readers and viewers encounter it, but I hope my art always invites more than it contains.

Steven Schroeder is a visual artist and poet who lives and works in Chicago. More at stevenschroeder.org.
Steven Schroeder | stvnschrd@gmail.com |
stevenschroeder.org